"In today's culture, it is essential that ministry leaders have clarity from Scripture regarding God's love for children. This book brings together some of the greatest thought leaders in Baptist life to address the critical subject of children and salvation in a manner that is comprehensive, practical, and pastoral."

—**Adam Groza**, PhD, president, Gateway Seminary

"*Children & Salvation* equips readers with both theological depth and practical insight, fostering a well-rounded approach to discipling the next generation. Whether used in seminaries or the local church, this highly anticipated textbook is an essential resource that needs to be on the shelf of everyone involved in the spiritual formation of children. It is truly filling a gap in the understanding of how the gospel interacts with kids of all ages, making it invaluable for pastors, parents, and Nextgen leaders."

—**Jana Magruder**, strategic initiatives director, Lifeway NextGen

"In *Children & Salvation,* Karen Kennemur, Kelly A. King, Shelly Melia, and Donna B. Peavey provide a theologically rich and practical guide to assist in creating a framework for how your church thinks about children, the gospel, and salvation. The mosaic formed in this book gives an essential set of topics to help you align faithful theology with a practical approach to reaching and discipling today's kids. From a biblical basis, to children with disabilities, to evangelism, baptism, family, and discipleship—this book has it all. A must-read for any church leader!"

—**Matt Markins**, president and CEO, Awana

"*Children & Salvation* is a must-read for anyone serious about leading the next generation to Jesus. Karen Kennemur, Kelly A. King, Shelly Melia, and Donna B. Peavey have put together a resource that is both biblically sound and incredibly practical. They tackle big questions—What does the Bible say about children and salvation? How do we share the gospel with kids? What about baptism, discipleship, and even children with disabilities?—all with clarity, conviction, and a deep love for seeing young hearts transformed by Jesus. If you're a parent, pastor, or leader looking for a rock-solid guide to helping kids know and follow Christ, this book needs to be on your shelf!"

—**Shane Pruitt**, PhD, national next gen director, North American Mission Board

"*Children & Salvation* is a vital resource that connects biblical scholarship with practical ministry application. Grounded in Scripture and theological insight, this work empowers pastors, family ministers, children's leaders, and parents to engage in the important conversations surrounding a child's faith journey. Authored by respected Christian scholars, it clarifies foundational topics such as evangelism, discipleship, and baptism for children. This book is an indispensable tool for those seeking to faithfully guide the next generation in their understanding of salvation."

—**Adam Wright**, president, Dallas Baptist University

CHILDREN & SALVATION

CHILDREN & SALVATION

Biblical, Theological, AND Practical Considerations

Karen Kennemur, Kelly A. King, Shelly Melia, *and* Donna B. Peavey

B&H ACADEMIC®
BRENTWOOD, TENNESSEE

Children and Salvation: Biblical, Theological, and Practical Considerations

Published by B&H Academic®
Brentwood, Tennessee

ISBN: 979-8-3845-1060-4

Dewey Decimal Classification: 248.82
Subject Heading: CHILDREN--RELIGIOUS
LIFE \ SALVATION \ CHILDREN

Cover design by Emily Keafer Lambright. Cover illustration sourced from Gokcemim/iStock and Grafikactiva/iStock.

Printed in the United States of America
30 29 28 27 26 25 VP 2 3 4 5 6 7 8 9 10

CONTENTS

INTRODUCTION

Karen Kennemur

Only two academic books have been written on children and salvation from the Baptist perspective. In 1953, Broadman Press published *Winning the Children* by Gaines Dobbins, dean of the School of Religious Education of Southern Baptist Theological Seminary. In his book, he stated, "The winning of the children to Christ is not incidental. It is today's supreme imperative." He went on to say, "The spiritual law, that God uses human instrumentality to accomplish his saving purpose, operates in the winning of children no less than in the winning of adults."[1]

In 1970, Clifford Ingle led a group of seminary and university professors who collaborated on the book *Children and Conversion,* published by Broadman Press. Ingle believed this to be the first work of its kind—multiple authors on this topic—produced by Baptists. It was considered "pioneer work." The subject of children and salvation was "approached from a wider and more balanced perspective than any one author could provide."[2]

---

[1] Gaines Dobbins, *Winning the Children* (Broadman: 1953), 2.
[2] Clifford Ingle, *Children and Conversion* (Broadman: 1970), 8.

This writing is to carry on the tradition of the book *Children and Conversion. Children and Salvation* was written by Baptist seminary and university professors. At the time of the writing, these professors are some of the most learned people in their fields. The table of contents reads like a Who's Who list or a sports league all-star roster. The hope and prayer of the authors is to highlight the importance of sharing the gospel with children, discipling children, and including children as a vital part of the Christian community.

Our hope is that all pastors, ministers of various ministries, and seminary and university students, will prepare to succinctly lead children to their own faith in Christ, continually guide them in discipleship, and actively model the life of Christ.

CHAPTER 1

Children in the Old Testament

Joshua E. Williams

The Old Testament (OT) is the foundation for a Christian understanding of who God is and what he is like. The OT claims and illustrates that the Lord God is the one who creates, blesses, curses, commands, judges, provides, forgives, promises, directs, saves, and much more. Within the OT there is a repeated confession regarding the nature and character of the Lord: "The Lord—the Lord is a compassionate and gracious God, slow to anger and abounding in faithful love and truth, maintaining faithful love to a thousand generations, forgiving iniquity, rebellion, and sin. But he will not leave the guilty unpunished, bringing the consequences of the fathers' iniquity on the children and grandchildren to the third and fourth generation" (Exod 34:6–7). This confession reveals the merciful yet just character of God. However, the final part of the confession seems out of place for many contemporary readers. Why would God bring down the consequences of one generation's sins on even the third or fourth generation? Did such a thing really happen in the OT? Was it limited to adults who committed sins, or did it extend even to their children who did not?

The story of Achan (Joshua 7) provides some answers to the question. When Achan violated the ban of gathering spoils from Jericho, not only did Achan pay the penalty, but the rest of his household did as well, including his children: "Then Joshua, together with all Israel, took Achan son of Zerah, the silver, the robe, the gold bar, his sons and daughters, his cattle, donkeys and sheep, his tent and all that he had, to the Valley of Achor. Joshua said, 'Why have you brought this trouble on us? The Lord will bring trouble on you today.' Then all Israel stoned him, and after they had stoned the rest, they burned them" (Josh 7:24–25 NIV). The father's sin cost his entire household their lives.

This narrative raises many questions, but an important question is: How does such a picture make sense of God's justice and mercy? Part of the answer to that question involves the role of covenants in God's relationship to humankind, including children. Understanding the role of covenants in the OT is important when addressing the place of children within God's designs.

The Covenant and the Divine-Human Relationship in the Old Testament

In simple terms, a covenant is a formalized, legal agreement between parties.[1] Covenants governed relationships, establishing the expectations,

[1] At times, the OT uses the language of covenant to describe informal arrangements (e.g., 2 Chron 23:1); however, within the essay, only formal covenants are in view.

responsibilities, benefits, and consequences among the participants.[2] When people agreed to a covenant, they were determining how the relationship would look. The covenant spelled out the responsibilities for each party of the covenant. Therefore, the participants knew what to expect from themselves and each other. The covenant also spelled out the benefits for keeping the covenant and the penalties for breaking it. The covenant provided a clear, legal, formal means of regulating a relationship among the participants.

God established a covenant with the people of Israel at Mount Sinai. Exodus 19 records Israel's initial encounter with the Lord there. The focus of this covenant is clearly the nation: Verses 5–6 describe Israel as "my own possession," "a kingdom of priests," and "a holy nation" if they will obey the Lord's voice and covenant. The remainder of the Lord's encounter with Israel at Sinai continues the same focus on the nation of Israel. Even the end of Leviticus describes what the Lord said at Sinai as "the commandments that the Lord commanded Moses for the people of Israel" (Lev 27:34 ESV).

The covenant regulates the relationship between the Lord and Israel. One may summarize that relationship as follows: The Lord is Israel's God and Israel is the Lord's people (see, e.g., Exod 6:7; Lev 26:12; Jer 30:22; Ezek 36:28). This expression of the relationship carries numerous implications with it. One such implication

---

[2] The topic of covenant has been a major theme within Old Testament studies. For a helpful, brief treatment of some of the key questions regarding covenants, see William J. Dumbrell, *Covenant and Creation: A Theology of Old Testament Covenants* (Thomas Nelson, 1984), 15–20. For a brief summary of scholarly interaction on covenant in the OT, see Ellen Juhl Christiansen, *The Covenant in Judaism and Paul: A Study of Ritual Boundaries as Identity Markers*, Arbeiten zur Geschichte des antiken Judentums und des Urchristentums 27 (E. J. Brill, 1995), 4–8.

is that Israel has a special obligation to worship the Lord as God. Even though all nations should acknowledge the Lord as God, Israel does so in unique ways. For instance, the Lord chose Israel to construct a tabernacle, followed by a temple, for his worship. Furthermore, for Israel to be the Lord's people carries numerous implications as well. One implication is that, even though the Lord is concerned with all nations, he is concerned with Israel in special ways. For instance, the Lord gave Israel the law through Moses, including many commandments specifically applicable to them (e.g., festival celebrations). Therefore, the covenant served as an important means of setting out clearly what was expected and required from the Lord and from Israel. The covenant also established the benefits and penalties for either obeying or disobeying the covenant stipulations.

Implications of Covenant for Divine-Human Relationship

God's Salvation in a Covenant Context

The paradigmatic act of God's salvation in the OT is the exodus from Egypt.[3] In this great act, the Lord delivered the people of Israel from Egyptian bondage to bring them to Mount Sinai where he established a covenant with them. The OT deliverance illustrates two important points regarding God's relationship to humankind. First, the salvation in view is a national salvation for all Israel. The

[3] For a helpful, brief look at the importance and significance of the exodus, see Eugene Merrill, "The Meaning and Significance of the Exodus Event," in *Reverberations of the Exodus in Scripture*, ed. R. Michael Fox (Pickwick, 2014): 14–17.

paradigmatic act of salvation is not the salvation of an individual but the salvation of the whole nation. Although the OT addresses individual salvation, its focus is most often on corporate salvation. Second, the exodus as an act of salvation is an act of earthly deliverance. Although there are spiritual elements associated with the exodus (e.g., judgment on the Egyptian gods, Exod 12:12), the deliverance is a physical one from physical slavery and physical suffering. Within the OT's covenantal structure, such an emphasis on the earthly blessings makes sense.

The earthly blessings of the covenant included success in battle, peace and security in their land, fruitfulness in their fields and among their livestock, and children (see Leviticus 26 and Deuteronomy 26). Children are the key to maintaining the future of the nation as a people, the land that they inhabit, and the covenant between the Lord and them. Without children, the nation would suffer extinction, the land that God promised them would be left to others, and the covenant that God made would no longer apply.[4] Unlike many in contemporary Western cultures, the people within the OT were deeply concerned with preserving the memory and the land of their ancestors (for instance, see the laws regarding levirate marriage in Deuteronomy 25 and kinsman redemption in Leviticus 25). As a result, children held tremendous value for Israel as the people of God. Therefore, the OT encourages parents to train their children in their covenant obligations for the well-being and future preservation of the nation (e.g., Deut 4:9–10; 6:4–9; 11:18–21).

---

[4] Beyond the physical survival of the people, OT texts point to children's role in the cultural (often theological) survival of the family and nation; see Laurel Koepf-Taylor, *Give Me Children or I Shall Die: Children and Communal Survival in Biblical Literature*, Emerging Scholars (Fortress, 2013), 70–91.

Corporate and Individual Responsibility Within the Covenant

Since the Lord made a covenant with Israel as a nation, the focus of much of the OT is on the nation and how God relates to numerous individuals through the framework of that national covenant. Most often, those individuals carry some form of authority over the people because of the special roles they occupy. For instance, the OT records much about the kings who ruled over the people of Israel. When one examines the accounts of the kings, one notices that the actions of a king have a predictable effect on the nation. Obedient kings bring about good circumstances for the nation, while disobedient kings bring about bad circumstances for the nation. Within a covenantal structure, this connection makes sense. As an authority over the people, the king brings blessing or curse, benefit or disaster.[5] Therefore, when Asa did what was right and destroyed the symbols of false worship, all the nation experienced peaceful security (2 Chron 14:1–5). At the same time, when David ordered a sinful census, thousands perished (2 Sam 24:1–15; 1 Chron 21:1–14).

Even though the OT focuses on the corporate element of God's relationship with humankind, many passages deal with individual elements as well. The corporate element recognized how a person's actions, especially a person with authority, could impact the larger group. However, is it just for one generation to disobey and the next generation to pay the price? The OT addresses this question.

---

[5] The connection between the king and nation was not unique to ancient Israel. In fact, as Knoppers states, it "reflects a cardinal tenet of ancient Near Eastern royal ideology, that a people may experience weal or woe contingent upon the standing of its king with the divine realm." See Gary Knoppers, *I Chronicles 10–29: A New Translation with Introduction and Commentary*, The Anchor Bible 12A (Doubleday, 2004), 755.

Within the Mosaic law, (that is, the law delivered through Moses), God commanded that a son should not be executed for his father's sins and that a father should not be executed for his son's sins (Deut 24:16). Therefore, whatever consequences a son might suffer because of his father's sins, they did not include his execution. In the context of the exile, Ezekiel (Ezekiel 18) took up the question as well. The new generation complained that their ancestors committed the sins but that this generation was suffering the punishment. Ezekiel spoke to that new generation what the Lord revealed: "Look, every life belongs to me. The life of the father is like the life of the son—both belong to me. The person who sins is the one who will die" (v. 4). These two statements (the law and the prophetic oracle) help qualify the corporate elements of covenant and show that the relationship between the corporate and individual is complex within the OT.[6]

To illustrate this complex relationship, one can look to one account of King Jehoram's reign (2 Chronicles 21). Jehoram contracted an excruciating, deadly disease because he murdered his brothers and rejected the Lord (vv. 11–15, 18–19). God punished Jehoram individually because of his sins. However, at the same time, the narrative depicts a corporate element because Jehoram's sins also led to the people's sins as they followed him (vv. 11, 13). The result was not merely personal punishments for each individual's sin but national punishments as the nation lost power in the region (Edom and Libnah revolted, vv. 8–10) and foreign invaders attacked and captured

---

[6] For a fuller discussion regarding how the corporate and individual elements operate in the OT, see Joel S. Kaminsky, *Corporate Responsibility in the Hebrew Bible* (T&T Clark, 1995; paperback edition, 2019), 179–89. Citations refer to paperback edition.

many of the people, including Jehoram's wives and children (v. 17). The corporate and individual elements have a complex interplay.

The Agency of Children Within the Covenant

Even as the example of Jehoram illustrates, the place of children within this complex relationship of corporate and individual elements is usually one-sided. Because of Jehoram's wickedness, foreign invaders captured his children and took them away. They were victims, not agents. In fact, the OT does not directly address the question of agency for children; that is, it does not address what decisions a child can or should make, nor at what age they can or should do so. In fact, in nearly every passage that mentions children, the agency is almost entirely that of adults.

Even though the OT does not focus on the agency of children, there are some passages that touch on the question. The account of King Josiah recorded in 2 Chronicles serves as a positive example (34:1–35:27). At the start of the account, the text says that Josiah began to seek the God of his ancestor David during the eighth year of his reign, while he was still a youth, at sixteen years of age (34:3). In this passage, seeking God involved deliberate decisions of devotion to God. In other words, when Josiah was sixteen years old, he chose to devote himself exclusively to the Lord. As a result, he would worship only the Lord. At least by that age, Josiah could make such a commitment. At twenty years of age, he began instituting religious reforms throughout the land. Perhaps by that point, Josiah was considered an adult.[7] Nevertheless, God considered Josiah's devotion

[7] The OT does not specify an age of adulthood; however, at twenty years old, males could fulfill certain military and priestly roles; see Joshua E.

proper and rewarded Josiah for his actions that followed that devotion (vv. 2; 27–28). As a result, the passage suggests that, at least for Josiah, he was capable of and responsible for making such a spiritual decision by the age of sixteen.

Another passage that touches on the question is the account of Elisha and a group of harassing children (2 Kgs 2:23–25). The passage describes a group of children who harass the prophet Elisha by crying out, "Go up, baldy! Go up, baldy!" Elisha faces them and curses them in the name of the Lord. Immediately following, two female bears emerge from the woods and maul people in the group. Even though for most contemporary readers this passage is quite strange, still, three observations regarding the narrative may help explain how it addresses the topic of children and their agency. First, the terminology used to describe the children's activity indicates something much more severe than simple teasing. The activity involves the type of derision that kings have for a city before conquering its defenses (Hab 1:9–10) or that foreigners have for a nation condemned because of its bloodthirstiness (Ezek 22:4–5).[8] Second, the group of children must have been quite large, consisting of at least forty-two children (the language of the text implies a larger number). It makes sense that Elisha could interpret such a large group of those harassing him as a significant insult (to himself and God) and a considerable physical threat to himself.[9] Third, the text does not address their ages. Numerous interpreters understand

---

Williams and Calvin F. Pearson, *1 & 2 Chronicles: A Commentary for Biblical Preaching and Teaching*, Kerux Commentaries (Kregel, 2024), 536.

[8] Julie Faith Parker, *Valuable and Vulnerable: Children in the Hebrew Bible, Especially the Elisha Cycle*, Brown Judaic Studies 355 (Brown Judaic Studies, 2013), 94.

[9] Parker, 99.

this group to be composed of older youths, or, perhaps even better, younger adults. However, generally, the terminology used to describe the group refers to younger children, perhaps anywhere from about five to thirteen years old.[10] Furthermore, nothing in the context suggests that the terminology carries a sense outside its typical usage, except for the severe consequences of the individuals' actions. The descriptions of the activity and size of the group demonstrate that, even if the group consisted of smaller children, it would require some type of significant response.

Considering the above observations, it is not entirely surprising that Elisha takes action against the group. However, if this group is composed of children, then one wonders whether they can be held accountable for their actions. It seems that most people in the contemporary Western context would argue that they cannot; however, as Parker states, "the text (along with Elisha and YHWH [the Lord]) holds them completely liable."[11] As a result, this narrative does address the agency of children and shows that, at least in some cases, they are to be held accountable for their actions, especially when acting independently.

---

[10] Although it is common to associate childhood with certain ages, more likely other factors played a role in identifying a person as a child. For instance, Eng states that a young child would refer to "a young person below puberty but above the age of an infant or weaned child." Milton Eng, *The Days of Our Years: A Lexical Semantic Study of the Life Cycle in Biblical Israel*, Library of Hebrew Bible/Old Testament Studies 464 (T&T Clark, 2011), 76. For a more detailed discussion of identifying childhood, see Kristine Henriksen Garroway, "Methodology: Who Is a Child and Where Do We Find Children in the Ancient Near East?" in *T&T Clark Handbook of Children in the Bible and the Biblical World*, ed. Sharon Betsworth and Julie F. Parker (T&T Clark, 2019), 67–74.

[11] Parker, *Valuable and Vulnerable*, 99.

Children as Members of the People of God

Since God made a covenant with the nation of Israel, then membership into that covenant entailed being a member of Israel. Because Israel was an ethnic, national people, generally an individual did not choose to be a member of the people; they were born into it or incorporated into it through adoption or marriage. At the same time, being a member of Israel did not make one right before God. Much of the OT narrative and prophetic books focus on how Israel's leaders and the rest of the people disobeyed what God required as specified in the covenant made at Sinai. As an example, 2 Chron 36:11–19 describes the final days of Judah before the Babylonian exile. The passage recounts how King Zedekiah did what was evil before God and how the other members of Judah's leadership and the people in general acted wickedly to arouse God's anger. At the same time, the text speaks of Judah as God's people. They were still members of Israel, but they were not righteous before God. Their activity led to exile from the land God had promised them and even threatened their status as the Lord's people. In one sense, because the Lord made a covenant with Israel, they were the Lord's people and would continue to be so until the covenant was nullified. In another sense, because they did not treat the Lord as their God, which is the heart of the covenant, at times, they were not his people (see, e.g., Hos 1:9). For most of their history, they worshipped other gods and ignored the obligations of the covenant, even though some individuals maintained their devotion to the Lord (e.g., Obadiah; 1 Kgs 18:3). Furthermore, at times, the people would renew their commitment to be the Lord's people by devoting themselves as a people to him (e.g., 2 Chron 23:16). These reflections indicate that being the Lord's people carried two senses: (1) being Israel as the Lord's chosen nation and (2) devoting themselves to the Lord. Keeping both senses in mind when considering Israel as the people of the Lord is important.

An obvious implication of this type of covenant membership is that Israelite children are members of God's people, at least in the sense of being members of God's chosen nation. For boys, the law required circumcision on the eighth day after birth to mark their membership within the covenant. Circumcision identified the boy as an Israelite and reminded him of his identity and responsibility as a member of God's people (see Gen 17:9–14).[12] It was not the responsibility of the infant boy to be circumcised but of others to circumcise him. Even without circumcision, the boy was still a member of the nation and thereby a member of the covenant community. However, refusing to be circumcised carried serious consequences and broke the covenant (v. 14).

Beyond circumcision, the OT records other instances in which children are dedicated to the Lord in a special way, often even before birth. Samson and Samuel serve as examples. Before Samson was born, the messenger of the Lord communicated to his parents that he would be a Nazirite from birth (Judg 13:5). This duty was bestowed on him from birth without his consent. In the context, the restrictions of the Nazirite relate to Samson's coming role as a

---

[12] Circumcision may have served numerous functions. The OT uses circumcision as a metaphor in many ways; however, one consistent aspect is that circumcision "connotes suitability for participation in what God is doing." *The Anchor Yale Bible Dictionary: A–C*, "Circumcision" (Yale University Press, 1992), https://www.theologyandreligiononline.com/encyclopedia?docid=b-9780300261875. See also the helpful, brief discussion in Gordon J. Wenham, *Genesis 16–50*, WBC 2 (Word Books, 1994), 23–24 and David A. Bernat, *Sign of the Covenant: Circumcision in the Priestly Tradition*, Ancient Israel and Its Literature 3 (SBL, 2009), 36–40.

savior for the people because "he will begin to save Israel from the power of the Philistines" (v. 5b). Samson did begin to deliver Israel until he violated all three Nazirite prohibitions. His choice to disregard his status as a Nazirite resulted in dire consequences for him. In a similar situation, Samuel's mother dedicated him to the Lord before he was born. As a result, Samuel served within the Lord's sanctuary even as a child although he did not receive any direct communication from the Lord until later (1 Sam 3:7). At the same time, Samuel's service within the sanctuary prepared him for his role as a prophetic figure leading the people of Israel to transition to the period of the monarchy. In both examples, the preparation and selection of the child did not involve bringing the child into the community of faith but selecting the child for a particular task within God's plan for his people.

Maintaining and Preserving the Covenant Through Rituals

Within the formal framework of the covenant, the OT most often depicts religious devotion in terms of practicing rituals. The OT regularly praises those who practice appropriate rituals or condemns those who practice illicit ones. Some rituals were performed regularly by individuals; however, other rituals were performed corporately, either at a national level or perhaps at the family level. Furthermore, the rituals were to be performed on a regular basis. For instance, Sabbath observance took place every week. Furthermore, the Sabbath functioned as a reminder both that God created the world (Exod 20:11) and that God delivered Israel from the bondage of slavery (Deut 5:15). The focus on rituals makes sense in the context because rituals like the Sabbath served as a standardized mode for honoring and preserving the covenant between the Lord and Israel.

The corporate nature of these rituals certainly resulted in not only adults participating but also children participating. The OT rarely mentions children, but since the ancient world contained more children than today's Western context, one would expect children to be all around and to be active members of communal life.[13] Furthermore, through their participation in rituals, children learned how to act properly in devotion to God. The rituals served as reminders both for the adults and for the children, reminders of who God is and what he has done. Perhaps no ritual illustrates this better than Passover. As Moses instructed the people how to protect themselves from the destroying angel who would pass throughout Egypt, he concluded his instructions with an exhortation to observe the ritual permanently from generation to generation, even when they settle in the land that God had promised them (Exod 12:24–25). Following his exhortation, he portrays a hypothetical situation in which one of the children asks about the meaning of the ritual. Moses commands the people to respond in the following way: "It is the Passover sacrifice to the Lord, for he passed over the houses of the Israelites in Egypt when he struck the Egyptians and spared our homes" (v. 27). Since the children participate in the ritual observance, they ask regarding its meaning. Their question indicates two aspects of the ritual: (1) through the ritual, the children learn to recognize the Lord's work by knowing their history and interpreting it properly as the Lord's activity on their behalf and (2) the ritual prompts the ethical demand for the

---

[13] Julie Faith Parker, "Children in the Hebrew Bible and Childist Interpretation," *Currents in Biblical Research* 17, no. 2 (2019): 131, http://journals.sagepub.com/doi/10.1177/1476993X18821324.

parents to "guide" their children in remembering and recognizing the Lord's work.[14]

Concluding Remarks on Children in the Old Testament

In seeking to understand how the OT speaks of children and their spiritual status before God, it is important to remember the covenantal nature of God's relationship with Israel. Because of that covenant, God's relationship with his people bears corporate and individual aspects. Corporately, God saved the nation, chose them, and granted them a special role among the nations of the world. He also obligated them to the terms of the covenant as a nation. If they obeyed it, God would bless them, but if they disobeyed it, God would punish them. At the same time, he obligated individuals to obey his commandments. God also rewarded and punished individuals based on their obedience or disobedience within the covenant.

The nature of the covenant with Israel also led to a focus on earthly blessings. Such blessings would include matters important for a nation: peaceful security throughout their land, prosperous fruitfulness of the land, and plenty of children to maintain possession of the land. Even the paradigmatic act of salvation, the exodus, was a salvation in earthly terms. As a result, one should be careful not to read other meanings of salvation (e.g., spiritual salvation) into OT passages about salvation without clear warrants for doing so.

---

[14] Dru Johnson, *Knowledge by Ritual: A Biblical Prolegomenon to Sacramental Theology*, Journal of Theological Interpretation Supplements 13 (Eisenbrauns, 2016), 246–47.

In describing the covenantal nature of God's relationship to Israel, one can see that, in many ways, children are no different from most adults when it comes to their membership in the covenant community and the effects of the community on their lives. Most adults lived under the authority of national leaders (e.g., kings) whose actions would affect their own fates, whether they lived obediently or disobediently before the Lord. Their membership in the community made them subject to national blessings and national disasters.

Many passages that portray God's judgment falling on children fall within the corporate aspects of the covenant. When the king or family leader commits a sin, sometimes the children suffer the consequences as well (e.g., the narrative of Achan in Joshua 7). At the same time, the Lord's work is just in ultimately ensuring that the soul that sins will die (Ezek 18:4). The interplay between the corporate and individual aspects of God's relationship to Israel is a rich and complex theological question.

Most OT passages do not show children as active agents. Most of the time, adults act on children, whether for their benefit or harm. At times, the OT records the actions of a child or group of children. In the case of Josiah, the OT records how he determined to devote himself to the Lord. In the case of the children mocking Elisha, the OT records how Elisha and the Lord held the children responsible for their actions. Although one should be careful not to make too much of a single example, the example does push against contemporary Western notions of children as either innocent or not morally culpable for their actions.

The OT addresses some examples in which children are dedicated to the Lord, sometimes even before birth. Two examples addressed above are Samson and Samuel. For Samson, God used him to begin to deliver the people from the Philistines. For Samuel,

God used him as a national, prophetic leader who would initiate the period of the monarchy by anointing Saul and then David. In both cases, the dedication related to the child's special role within God's plan for his people; it did not relate to membership in the covenant community.

Children were members of the covenant community because they were members of Israel. Therefore, even as children, they were members of God's chosen nation. However, as pointed out above, there is another sense in which the people of God are those who devote themselves to him. Regarding children, this point suggests that one should not draw a simple line between OT covenant membership and New Testament (NT) church membership. Who constitutes the people of God is an important question addressed in the NT. John 1:12–13 addresses the question. The passage points to faith in Christ, in contrast to one's natural heritage, as the qualifying characteristic of those adopted as children of God. Therefore, one must address the OT evidence carefully when drawing conclusions regarding children and their membership in the covenant community.

At the same time, children did participate in the routine rituals of the covenant community. Participation in the rituals reminded God's people of his character and work while it taught the children how to act properly in devotion to God. The participation of children in these rituals was necessary for preserving the covenant into the future. As a result, one should think carefully about how children participate within the life of contemporary churches. The picture of children participating in the regular rhythms of the covenant community so that they can learn who God is and what he has done may suggest that some type of analogous participation of children in the regular rhythms of contemporary church life is warranted and even encouraged for the instruction of the children and the future preservation of the church community.

In closing, the OT provides rich material for theological reflections on children. On one hand, children are usually not independent active agents, but their fates lie in the hands of others. On the other hand, the OT does not present children as simply innocent but, at least on occasion, as morally responsible. Even though children do not occupy a prominent role within the covenant, they occupy a highly valuable one. They are those instructed through the community's routine rhythms of rituals, and they are those who must preserve the covenant into the future.

Discussion Questions

1. What role should corporate awareness play in the theology and practice of today's churches? How might such corporate elements interplay with individual elements in theology and practice as well? What role do corporate and individual elements play in a theology of salvation and judgment?
2. What are Christian analogies to OT rituals? How do they differ? How are they the same? Should children participate in regular worship services, the Lord's Supper, or baptism? In what ways is it appropriate for children to be a part of a church congregation? In what ways is it inappropriate?
3. How does the OT push against contemporary conceptions of children? Compare your attitudes regarding the moral responsibility of children with the OT's view. What types of decisions do children make in the OT? When do they make such decisions? How should the OT's picture of children's

agency shape current views of the spiritual state of children and the practice of instructing them?

4. How do contemporary practices of dedicating children differ from the OT examples? Is there a place for dedicating children within contemporary churches? How does baptism compare to circumcision? What possible role might baptism serve for children?

Opportunities for Application

- Thinking about how the OT encourages parents to train their children in their covenant obligations for the well-being and future preservation of the nation, consider how your church includes children in corporate settings. List the different rituals or ordinances in your church where children could be observers if not participants. Develop a plan to include children in settings that prompt parents to guide their children in remembering and recognizing the Lord's work. How often could you include children in those settings? What resources could you develop or provide to guide parents in including children? What resources could you develop or provide to guide children before or during those occasions?
- Provide parents with resources to incorporate ways to remember the Lord's work through prayer and Bible reading in home settings.
- Provide resources for preschool and children's ministry leaders to encourage and reinforce the importance of prayer and Bible learning for boys and girls apart from their church

participation. Guide preschool and children's ministry leaders to support and encourage parents in their efforts at home to help their children remember and recognize the Lord's work.

- Guide a child to name things he can do for God as an individual and things he can do for God as part of a church.

CHAPTER 2

Children in the New Testament

James R. Wicker

The NT focuses on adults far more than it does on children. It was written by adults and mostly for adults. It describes Jesus's and the apostles' ministries, which mainly were to adults. Yet, the NT mentions children in every book except Jude,[1] and it gives important teachings about them. This chapter will examine what the NT teaches about (1) the value of children in society, (2) the familial role of children, (3) the importance of children in God's kingdom, and (4) the use of children as positive and negative spiritual examples.

[1] All but Jude refer to children literally or metaphorically. Considering Jude's brevity and subject matter, the lack of references to children is not surprising.

Who is a child? The NT uses the following terms: *brephos* ("unborn baby," "baby, "infant"), *nēpios* ("infant," "child," "minor"), *teknion* ("little child"), *teknon* ("child"), *pais* ("child," "boy," "son," "girl," "daughter"), *paidarion* ("child," "boy"), and *korasion* ("girl"). Also, *huios* ("son") and *thugatēr* ("daughter") can refer to a child. These ancient word meanings differ little from modern usage. Interestingly, there is no NT word for the modern teenager nor an equivalent to the modern delayed gap between childhood and adulthood. After childhood, one became an adult (1 Cor 13:11): at the age of twelve for a female, now a young woman (*neanis*),[2] and thirteen for a male, now a young man (*neanias*, Acts 7:58; 20:9; *neaniskos*, Matt 19:20; Acts 23:18).[3]

The Value of Children in Society

With modern Western society's vast focus on children, from designer babies to luxury baby clothes, from exclusive schools to elite sports clubs, it is hard to imagine how low children were in status in first-century AD Roman patriarchal society. They were overlooked and undervalued. They consumed family resources with little economic benefit, although older ones could do some work in the home and field as well as help look after the younger children at home.[4] Childhood death was common, and many did not live to see their

---

[2] *Neanis* is not in the NT, but it is in the Greek Septuagint translations of Exod 2:8; Ruth 2:5; 1 Kgs 1:4.

[3] J. Julius Scott Jr., *Jewish Backgrounds of the New Testament* (Baker, 1995), 249. He says those figures are approximate, but they seem to be fairly set for the Jews.

[4] Lynn Cohick, "Women, Children, and Families in the Greco-Roman World," in *The World of the New Testament: Cultural, Social, and Historical Contexts*, ed. Joel B. Green and Lee Martin McDonald (Baker Academic, 2013), 183.

first birthday due to the high mortality rate.[5] Their main worth was in their potential. When they became adults, they could contribute to society through work and continue a family into the next generation.

Jewish Families

Although Jewish families were patriarchal, they tended to value children more than did Gentile society.[6] Abortion and infanticide were common among Greeks and Romans but were forbidden by the Jews.[7] Jews had God's command to bear children (Gen 1:28),[8] who are in God's image (1:26–27; 9:6) and are God's blessing (Ps 127:3–5). Thus, childlessness brought multiple problems to a Jewish married couple: (1) disappointment, because it is a God-given desire for parents to want to bear children (1 Sam 1:2–11); (2) embarrassment, since people automatically assumed God was punishing the barren woman and husband (Lev 20:20–21; Jer 18:21); (3) disruption, since there was no male heir to inherit the couple's property (thus, the call for levirate marriage, Deut 25:5–10); and (4) danger, because a son was needed to financially care for aging parents (Ruth 1–2). However, bearing children was a blessing from God

---

[5] Some 30–35 percent lived only one month, and 50 percent did not live to the age of ten. Christian Laes, *Children in the Roman Empire: Outsiders Within* (Cambridge University Press, 2011), 26.

[6] For example, in P.Oxy. 744 a Greek Gentile named Hilarion wrote to his wife in 1 BC while he was away, "If by chance you bear a child, if it is a boy, let it be, if it is a girl, expose it." Everett Ferguson, *Backgrounds of Early Christianity*, 3rd ed. (Eerdmans, 2003), 81.

[7] For infanticide, see Tacitus, *Hist.* 5.5; Philo, *Special Laws* 3.110–19. For abortion, see Josephus, *Ag. Ap.* 2.202. Ferguson, *Backgrounds*, 80–82.

[8] Although God gave this command to Adam and Eve, it is for all humanity since Adam and Eve could not populate the earth on their own.

(Gen 1:28; 9:1) and a joyous occasion (Gen 21:6; 1 Sam 2:1–10). It was even more special to the elderly Zechariah and Elizabeth as well as to Joseph and Mary because of their sons' roles in God's salvific plan. There is great joy in Luke 1:14, 44; 2:10; and Matt 2:10.

God instructed the Jews to give children religious instruction in the home (Deut 6:1–9). This practice continued into first-century AD Palestine.[9] However, by that time, there was a local synagogue to help in the religious instruction of the sons.[10] Mothers taught their daughters at home. Families worshipped together on the Sabbath in the local synagogue (Luke 13:10; Acts 15:21), and there were many synagogues in Galilee (Mark 1:39) and Judea (Luke 4:44).[11]

Left Behind at the Temple (Luke 2:41–50)

Mary and Joseph were a righteous Jewish couple (Luke 1:28, 30, 38; Matt 1:19a). Being righteous included instructing children about God, as the Shema describes (Deut 6:4–9), and the rabbis affirm teaching the Torah to sons (b. Qidd. 29b). Jesus's parents reared him in Jewish teaching and practice, as reflected in the childhood story of

---

[9] Yinger says parents at home provided most Jewish education across Palestine in the first century AD. Kent L. Yinger, "Jewish Education," in *The World of the New Testament*, ed. Joel B. Green and Lee Martin McDonald (Baker Academic, 2013), 326–28.

[10] For teaching sons in a synagogue, see m. 'Abot 5:21; y. Meg. 3:1. For not teaching daughters in the synagogue, see b. Qidd. 29b. Edwin M. Yamauchi and Marvin R. Wilson, *Dictionary of Daily Life in Biblical and Post-Biblical Antiquity* (Hendrickson, 2015), "Education."

[11] There were 480 synagogues in Jerusalem before AD 70 according to y. Meg. 3:1. See E. M. Yamauchi, "Synagogues," in *Dictionary of New Testament Background*, ed. Craig A. Evans and Stanley E. Porter (InterVarsity, 2000). However, Yinger says this number may be exaggerated. Yinger, 327.

Jesus in Luke. The passage affirms some spiritual understanding of twelve-year-old Jesus. Granted, he was sinless (Heb 4:15) and thus unlike any other child his age. Yet, although he was fully divine (John 1:1), he was also fully human and developed physically and mentally like any other child, as indicated in the growth formulas about Jesus (Luke 2:40, 52).

Mary and Joseph traveled to Jerusalem annually for the Passover (v. 41), indicating they were Torah-observing Jews (see also vv. 21–24). Passover commemorated the tenth plague on Egypt and God's deliverance of the Jews from Egypt (Exod 12:1–36). Jewish men were to celebrate this feast annually (Exod 23:14–17; Lev 23:4–5), and they did so at the temple in Jesus's day. Jesus's parents took him with them to the temple for this feast when he was twelve years old (Luke 2:42), an important age for intensive religious teaching just before puberty.[12] This was Jesus's first Passover in Jerusalem that appears in the Gospels.

Jesus's family traveled in a caravan (v. 44), so the adults were often separated from the older children. Jewish pilgrims traveling in a group for fellowship and safety "functioned as a quasi-family (the Greek word for 'company,' *synodia*, sometimes means 'family')."[13] A caravan could include residents from one or more villages and be quite large.[14] This explains why they did not immediately notice Jesus was missing as they returned home. His parents found him

---

[12] A Jewish boy became a man at thirteen, at which age he became responsible for keeping the law. See m. Nid. 5:6; m. Meg. 4:6; James R. Edwards, *The Gospel According to Luke*, PNTC (Eerdmans, 2015), 92; Darrell L. Bock, *Luke* 1:1–9:50, BECNT (Baker Academic, 1994), 264.

[13] Edwards, 93.

[14] Alfred Plummer, *A Critical and Exegetical Commentary on the Gospel According to St. Luke*, ICC, 5th ed. (T&T Clark, 1989), 75.

"after three days" (v. 46). He was in the temple both listening to teachers and asking them questions. They were amazed at his answers (v. 47).

Jesus answered his parents' question of why he did this by saying, "I had to be in My Father's *house*" (v. 49 NASB). This shows some messianic consciousness of Jesus at this time in his life. "In identifying God as his Father, and in addressing God intimately and exclusively as '*my* Father,' Jesus fulfills the messianic ideal."[15] Scholars ponder at what point Jesus knew that he was the Messiah. Likely, it began at least by this time.

Age of Accountability

Many Baptists believe in a doctrine called the age of accountability.[16] This is the age when a person can understand his or her sinfulness and is thus responsible for this condition based on their willful choice of sin. Every human since Adam and Eve is conceived in sin (Rom 5:12; 1 Cor 15:22), meaning every person has a sin nature: a propensity to sin. Also, everyone willfully chooses to sin (Rom 3:23). Common sense indicates that an infant, toddler, and young child cannot understand sin nor the salvation Jesus offers. They can learn *what* the rules are at an early age, but they cannot yet understand the *why*: the purpose of rules and repercussions for disobedience. Yet, there comes a time when the child does understand the why, and it seems that is the time when the child becomes

---

[15] Edwards, *Luke*, 96.

[16] Millard J. Erickson, *Christian Theology*, 2nd ed. (Baker Academic, 1983), 654–56; E. Y. Mullins, *The Christian Religion in Its Doctrinal Expression* (Broadman, 1917), 301–2.

accountable.[17] When is this age? It probably is different for each person. Jesus had spiritual understanding by at least age twelve ("I must be about My Father's business," Luke 2:49 NKJV), and this was when Jewish parents intensified their religious teaching for their child. Perhaps this practice can give insight into when a child is accountable to God for his or her sins.[18] Of course, the age can be younger and likely is different for each child. Researcher George Barna notes some "two-thirds of all Americans who ever accept Jesus Christ as their Savior do so before the age of thirteen."[19]

The Bible is largely silent concerning whether a child who dies before reaching the age of accountability goes to heaven. The only scriptural support for the claim that they do may be when the child of David and Bathsheba died at seven days old. David said, "Can I bring him back again? [Answer: no.] I am going to him, but he will not return to me" (2 Sam 12:23 NASB). Most scholars believe David simply referred to death and said he will one day die. Yet, this writer believes David reflected a positive view of the afterlife since (1) "going to him" may indicate a personal reunion,[20] and (2) David

---

[17] Granted, there are no NT texts that specifically address the issue of infant salvation; however, Garrett notes there is a sound theological argument for the age of accountability that fits with those who propose believer's baptism rather than baptism of infants. James Leo Garrett Jr., *Systematic Theology: Biblical, Historical, and Evangelical*, vol. 1, 2nd ed. (Biblical Press, 2000), 580–87.

[18] Luke 2:52 says Jesus grew ethically, physically, spiritually, and socially. One should assume it was normal growth, albeit sinless. He never did any self-serving miracles, nor did he cheat in any way. Thus, it is reasonable to assume he did not preach as an infant, nor reach puberty at age six, nor think spiritual thoughts before any child would normally do so.

[19] George Barna, *Raising Spiritual Champions: Nurturing Your Child's Heart, Mind, and Soul* (Christian University Press, 2023), 7.

[20] Wayne Grudem, *Systematic Theology*, 2nd ed. (Zondervan, 2020), 631. He notes this passage addresses the child of a believer (David), not of an

reflected a similar optimistic view in some of his psalms (Ps 16:9–11; 41:12; and especially 23:6b, "My dwelling *will be* in the house of the LORD forever," emphasis added).[21]

Familial Role of Children

Many references to children in the NT mention them as part of a family unit. The four Gospels reflect life mostly in Jewish homes with occasional glimpses into Gentile families. In Acts, there is a transition from Jewish Christian homes to mostly Gentile Christian homes; yet both reflected similar values and roles for children (Acts 16:1; 2 Tim 1:15; 3:15, implying Timothy had religious instruction in the home). The early Christians were Jews who trusted in Christ, and OT moral values continued in NT believers, as is evident in the Christian household codes, such as Eph 5:22–6:9.

Family Members

The less important role of children in Jewish and Christian homes is evident in their omission from the count when Jesus fed five thousand men (Matt 14:21) and when he later fed four thousand men (15:38).[22] Many times, they are simply part of a family unit

---

unbeliever. See his larger discussion of the issue (629–31).

[21] Steven J. Lawson, *Psalms 1–75*, Holman OT Commentary (Holman Reference, 2003), 128.

[22] The five thousand were mostly Jewish, and the four thousand were mostly Gentile. Both Matthean passages say the number does not include women and children. Mark 6:44 does not mention women and children being absent in the count, but says it was *andres* ("men," and not likely "people" here). Mark 8:9 gives the masculine plural of four thousand (*tetrakischilioi*) for the other miraculous feeding.

(e.g., Acts 21:5; 1 Tim 5:14; Titus 1:6; and the household codes—see below).

As part of a family, children shared in the results of what their parents did, for good or ill:

1. In the parable of the unforgiving slave, a slave owing ten thousand talents was about to be sold for the debt along with his wife and children (Matt 18:25).
2. Children were part of the family of the man who refused to help until his friend was persistent in his request (Luke 11:7).
3. Jesus said his followers who left "houses or brothers or sisters or father or mother or children or farms" (Matt 19:29–30 NASB; see also Mark 10:29; Luke 18:29) for his sake will be rewarded many times over.
4. When the crowd repeatedly demanded Jesus's crucifixion and Pontius Pilate washed his hands of the matter, they responded, "His blood *shall be* on us and on our children" (Matt 27:25, emphasis added).[23]

Household Codes

Household codes were rules of conduct for how members of a household should relate to each other: the married couple, children, other relatives, and servants. These codes were common in Roman literature.[24] Household codes also appear in the NT, but they differ

[23] Through the years Jews have criticized this as an anti-Semitic remark inserted by Matthew; however, Matthew was a Jew himself. He simply recorded what happened.

[24] Cicero, *de Officiis* 1.139–41; Pliny the Elder, *Nat.* 7.1; Seneca, *Letters on Ethics: To Lucilius* 47.

from Roman society. First, Christian household codes have a strong emphasis that relationships should be reciprocal. For instance, there are obligations for children toward parents (Eph 6:1–3; Col 3:20) and fathers toward children (Eph 6:4; Col 3:21). Married couples have mutual obligations (Eph 5:22–31). Second, Christian household codes address children.[25] Since these NT letters were read to the congregation, these references indicate children gathered with their families for worship.[26] Third, there is a common equality among the members of a household. This was a revolutionary concept because it recognized the worth of what society otherwise saw as weak and less valued members of the household: women, children, and servants. Examples of Christian household codes appear in Eph 5:22–6:9; Col 3:18–4:1; 1 Pet 2:11–3:12; 1 Tim 2:8–15; 5:1–2; 6:1–2; and Titus 2:1–10; 3:1.

Childhood Roles

Two household codes in the NT specifically address children: Eph 6:1–4 and Col 3:20–21. They both affirm the worth and role of children simply by mentioning them in these household codes, which Roman codes do not do. In both passages, Paul said children must "obey" (*hupakouete*) their parents, saying, "for this is right" in Eph 6:1 (NASB) and, "for this is pleasing to the Lord" in Col 3:20 (NASB). In Eph 6:2, he cited the fifth commandment (Exod 20:12) in which children are to honor their parents. What is the difference between obedience and honor? Obedience is "to follow

[25] Roman household codes did not address children and just assumed their obedience. Benjamin L. Merkle, *Ephesians*, EGGNT (B&H Academic, 2016), 195.

[26] Merkle, 196.

instructions,"[27] so it makes sense that a child will do this until he or she moves out of the home as an adult and establishes a separate home (Gen 2:24). Obedience stops, but honor never ends.[28] Honor (*timaō*) means "to show high regard for," "revere."[29] A child should never stop honoring his or her parents, just as the fifth commandment says.

What about the promise of the fifth commandment, the "first commandment with a promise" (Eph 6:2)? In Exod 20:12 it says, "That your days may be prolonged on the land which the Lord your God gives you" (NASB). God gave the land of Canaan to the Jews in perpetuity; however, whether each generation was able to stay there depended on their obedience to God (Deuteronomy 27–28). Ephesians was a circular letter written to churches of Galatia, the main one being Ephesus. Ephesus was made up of both Jewish and Gentile Christians, so this OT promise given to Jews in the old covenant was not directly applicable. The promise was updated to something applicable to all Christians, "That you may live long on the earth" (Eph 6:3 NASB).

Parental Teaching and Care

Fathers must rear their children "in the discipline [*paideia*] and instruction [*nouthesia*] of the Lord" (Eph 6:4 NASB). *Paideia* means

[27] Frederick W. Danker et al., *Greek-English Lexicon of the New Testament and Other Early Christian Literature*, 3rd ed. (University of Chicago Press, 2000), *hypakouō*.

[28] Granted, the newly married couple did not always move to a new house. It was not uncommon in the Mediterranean world for multiple generations to live in the same house.

[29] BDAG, *timaō*.

"providing guidance for responsible living,"[30] such as in "discipline." *Nouthesia* is "counsel about avoidance or cessation of an improper course of conduct,"[31] such as "admonition." The emphasis of this latter term is more on "verbal correction."[32] So, these terms include Christian teachings of right and wrong.

Paul told fathers not to "provoke your children to anger" (Eph 6:4 NASB) and not to exasperate (*erithizete*, "stir up") them (Col 3:21). Why did he not include mothers in this imperative? The father was the primary disciplinarian in a first-century Jewish or Christian home. This was a warning not to be excessive, because Roman law may have allowed a father to punish a child to death.[33] Another aspect is not to annoy. Dads often like to tell corny jokes, play pranks, act silly, or kid a child (or his wife) simply to get a reaction out of them. When the children are small, they might find it funny. However, as they get older, they may get exasperated or irritated: "Dad, please stop!" Or they become the joke police, "That was not funny, Dad."

Jesus mentioned a father's kindness in teaching about prayer and the need to ask God for one's needs. He illustrated it with how a father is kind to his son and gives him good gifts. If a son asks his father for bread, he will not give him a stone. Nor will the father give him a snake instead of a fish (Matt 7:9–10).[34] Yet, God's gifts to his

---

[30] BDAG, *paideia*. See 1 Clem. 35:8; 56:16.

[31] BDAG, *nouthesia*. See Philo *Deus Imm.* 54; Josephus *Ant.* 3:11.

[32] Merkle, *Ephesians*, 198.

[33] Gaius, *Instit.* 1.5–59; Seneca, *De Clem.* 1.15.1–2; Cicero, *De Repub.* 1.38–39. However, the right of his power over life and death is debated today. See Cohick, "Women, Children," 180.

[34] Luke records when Jesus gave a similar illustration later, during the journey to Jerusalem. He used the fish and snake, but he also said a father will

children are even greater (v. 11), and these are examples of Jesus's teachings of the lesser to the greater.

The Value of Children in God's Kingdom

The two most important children in the NT are Jesus and John the Baptist. They are key to God's salvific plan, and Matthew and Luke each contain two chapters about their births.[35] They focus on God's call and preparation for Jesus's incarnation and resulting events. The emphasis on who John and Jesus are and the descriptions of their births highlight their important roles in this unique time in history. Their special births fulfill OT prophecy and show God's calling on them even while in the womb.

John the Baptist's Birth

Much of Luke 1 focuses on the prophecy and fulfillment of the birth of John the Baptist, the forerunner of the Messiah. Gabriel prophesied the birth to an incredulous Zechariah (vv. 5–23). His wife, Elizabeth, stayed secluded during the first six months of her pregnancy (vv. 24–25). Her "relative" (*syngenis*, v. 36) Mary visited her (vv. 39–45),[36] and John leaped in his mother's womb (v. 41), a

---

not give a scorpion instead of an egg (Luke 11:11–12).

[35] John's prologue (John 1:1–5) refers to God and the Word "in the beginning" (v. 1). However, there is no description of any events of Jesus's birth or childhood in Mark or John.

[36] Sometimes this word is translated "cousin." It means "relative" or "kinswoman." Since Mary was likely in her early teens and Elizabeth was "advanced in years" (Luke 1:18 ESV), beyond normal childbearing age, they were probably a generation or two apart in age.

miracle and affirmation of life in the womb. Mary sang a song of praise to God, called the *Magnificat* (vv. 46–55), and stayed three months (v. 56). John was born (vv. 57–66), and Zechariah sang a song of blessing, called the *Benedictus* (vv. 67–79). The chapter concludes with a Lukan growth formula about John. He grew, was "strong in spirit," and the "deserts" were his home until his public ministry (v. 80 NASB). The importance of children is evident in part of the prophesied role of John the Baptist, as told by Gabriel to Zechariah, "TO TURN THE HEARTS OF THE FATHERS BACK TO THEIR CHILDREN (v. 17 NASB)."

Jesus's Birth

Luke records only four infancy/childhood events about Jesus. All show his importance even as a child: (1) his circumcision (2:21); (2) his firstborn temple presentation, where both Simeon and Anna affirmed Jesus's messiahship (vv. 22–38); (3) the brief visit in Nazareth (v. 39); and (4) his temple visit at the age of twelve (vv. 41–50). However, Matthew mentions the visit of the magi, which occurred up to two years later.[37] This event affirms Jesus's importance by (1) the magi's reference to him as the "King of the Jews" (Matt 2:2 NASB), (2) the great distance they traveled (up to nine hundred miles), (3) the miraculous "star in the east" (vv. 2, 9–10 NASB) that guided them, and (4) their expensive gifts: gold, frankincense, and myrrh (v. 11).

---

[37] Since Herod had the Bethlehem boys who were two years old and younger slaughtered, Jesus's birth was no earlier than two years prior and likely less than one year, given Herod's likely addition of time for a margin of error in the ages of babies they murdered.

Jesus Healing Children

Jesus demonstrated his love for children and their value by his healings. He ministered to two girls on both sides of the Jewish social spectrum. He brought back to life the twelve-year-old daughter of Jairus, a synagogue official (Matt 9:18–26; Mark 5:21–43; Luke 8:40–56)—whose family was of high social status among Jews. He also healed the demonized daughter, a "child" (*paidion*, Mark 7:30) of a Syrophoenician woman (Matt 15:21–28; Mark 7:24–30)—a family of Gentiles, whom the Jews considered "dogs" (*kynaria*, Mark 7:28).[38] Jesus brought back to life a widow's dead son (a "young man," *neaniskos*, Luke 7:14) and healed a royal official's son who was near death (John 4:46–54). He healed a demon-possessed boy who often had seizures and fell into the fire or in water (Matt 17:14–18). Each of these healings were no doubt times of rejoicing. At Troas, Paul healed Eutychus after his deadly fall from a third-floor window (Acts 20:7–12). He is described as a "young man" (*neanias*, Acts 20:9) and a "boy" (*paida*, v. 12).

Bringing Children to Jesus (Matt 19:13–15; Mark 10:13–16; Luke 18:15–17)

Probably the most well-known event involving Jesus and children is when parents brought their "children" (*paidia*, Matt 19:13; Mark 10:13) and "even their babies" (*autō kai ta brephē*, Luke 18:15 NASB) to Jesus for him to "lay His hands on them and pray" (Matt 19:13 NASB). The disciples reflected the first-century AD attitude of marginalizing children, who had a low place in society. "Childhood

---

[38] When Jesus used this pejorative term with the woman, he was likely testing her faith, and she impressively passed (Matt 15:28).

was typically regarded as an unavoidable interim between birth and adulthood."[39] So, they rebuked the parents who tried to bring their children to Jesus. They probably thought Jesus was too important to be bothered.

However, Jesus was "indignant" (*ēganaktēsen*—a strong emotion, Mark 10:14) toward the disciples and told them to "permit" (*aphete*) the children to come to him. He showed they were worthy of his love and blessing.[40] This act exhibits their value to God and is an example for all people to follow in loving and ministering to children.

Jesus gave two important statements about them. First, "The kingdom of God belongs to such as these" (Mark 10:14b; Luke 18:16b NASB; cf. Matt 19:14b). How does it belong to them? They are able to enter it—at least the older ones can, the ones who can understand the gospel and make a faith commitment to Jesus. Second, "Truly I say to you, whoever does not receive the kingdom of God like a child will not enter it at all" (Mark 10:15; Luke 18:17 NASB). One "receives" the kingdom of God as a gift; thus, there is no way to earn salvation. How does one receive it "like a child"? Some scholars say Jesus referred to a child's characteristics, such as helplessness, obedience, or faith.[41] Others believe Jesus focused on

---

[39] James R. Edwards, *The Gospel According to Mark*, PNTC (Eerdmans, 2002), 306.

[40] The KJV translation here sounds frightening. Jesus said to "suffer" the children (Mark 10:14). Here is an example of how English has changed since 1611, because back then "suffer" could mean "permit" (NASB 1995).

[41] Robert H. Stein, *Mark*, BECNT (Baker Academic, 2008), 463–64; Darrell L. Bock, *Luke 9:51–24:53*, BECNT (Baker Academic, 1996), 1471. One should avoid using *every* quality of a child here, which would be an exegetical fallacy called illegitimate totality transfer. It involves bringing *every* characteristic of a referent into the meaning of a word and goes beyond the context of the passage. D. A. Carson, *Exegetical Fallacies*, 2nd ed. (Baker, 1996), 60–61.

a child's low social status of humbleness.[42] The latter interpretation better fits the context since the apostles appeared to devalue the children's worth, and Jesus did not mention any specific trait of children here.[43]

Children as Part of God's Plan

At times, a child had a key role in God's plan, demonstrating the value of children to God. It was a "boy" (*paidarion*, John 6:9) who provided the five loaves and two fish Jesus used to miraculously feed the crowd of five thousand men (vv. 10–11). Paul's nephew, a "young man" (*neanian*), warned Paul about the nefarious plot against his life, resulting in a large armed escort safely delivering Paul to Caesarea Maritima (Acts 23:12–23). Rhoda, the "servant-girl" (*paidiskē*), informed the people at Mary's house that their prayers were answered because Peter was at the gate, which she forgot to open (12:13–14). Yet, children can also work against God. The girl (*korasion*, Mark 6:22, 28) Salome did her mother's evil bidding and requested the head of John the Baptist, resulting in his martyrdom (vv. 25–29). A demonized slave girl (*paidiskēn*, Acts 16:16) disrupted Paul's mission work for many days until Paul exorcised the demon (v. 18).

---

[42] R. T. France, *The Gospel of Matthew*, NICNT (Eerdmans, 2007), 677–79, 727–28; Edwards, *Luke*, 509–10.

[43] Could the disciples simply have been concerned about Jesus's busy schedule without any negative attitude toward children? That is doubtful because (1) nowhere else in the Gospels did they try to prevent Jesus from ministering to someone, (2) the disciples "rebuked" the parents (Matt 19:13; Mark 10:13; Luke 18:15 NASB)—overkill if it is just a time issue—(3) Jesus's time or busyness is absent in the context, and (4) the idea of children as a worthy example does appear in the context.

Baptizing a Household

There are three instances in Acts where a "household" (*oikos*) trusted in Jesus and was baptized: Lydia (Acts 16:14–15), the Philippian jailer (vv. 30–34), and Crispus the synagogue leader at Corinth (18:8). The following should be assumed about these events. First, they were baptized *after* they trusted in Jesus (see 16:31; 18:8), as is the case in other NT passages (Matt 28:19; Acts 2:38, 41; 8:12–13). Second, no unbelievers and no infants or babies were baptized, because there is no NT evidence of such practice. One's trust in Jesus for salvation (John 3:16) always preceded the public testimony of baptism.

Children and Discipleship

Paul and Timothy are a great example of one-on-one discipleship. Paul called Timothy his "true son in *the* faith" (1 Tim 1:2 NASB) and "my beloved son" (2 Tim 1:2 NASB), likely meaning God used Paul's preaching/teaching to lead Timothy to trust in Jesus. Timothy was Paul's spiritual child. Yet, Paul noted the importance of the spiritual upbringing Timothy had at home from his Christian mother, Eunice, and grandmother, Lois (v. 5), who taught him "from childhood . . . the sacred writings" (3:15 NASB). Timothy joined Paul on his second missionary journey (Acts 16:1) as a valuable coworker who became a "kindred spirit" (Phil 2:20 NASB). When Timothy was pastor at Ephesus, Paul wrote the pastoral letters 1–2 Timothy to him.[44]

---

[44] Although neither letter explicitly says Timothy was the pastor of that church, this is the assumption based on the following verses implying a leadership position there: (1) Paul telling Timothy to remain at Ephesus to "instruct certain people" (1 Tim 1:3 NASB), (2) the command not to neglect

Children as Examples

Most NT references to children are positive. This is understandable—especially to readers who are parents or grandparents! What is not to love in those cute bundles of joy?

Children Praising Jesus (Matt 21:15)

Here is an example of children outshining some bitter Jewish leaders. Matthew and Mark record Jesus going to the temple on Sunday of the Passion Week, but only Matthew records what happened. Even the children proclaimed Jesus as Messiah. They cried out, "Hosanna to the Son of David," using a distinctive messianic title (Matt 21:15 NASB). The chief priests and scribes were "indignant" (v. 15). Jesus chided them in verse 16 for reading yet not understanding Psalm 8:2, "From the mouth of infants and nursing babies You have established strength" (NASB). God is so powerful that he uses the lowliest people to praise him.

Who Is the Greatest? (Matt 18:1–5; Mark 9:33–37; Luke 9:46–48)

Children can be an example of how to follow Christ. The disciples were arguing about "which of them might be the greatest" (Luke 9:46 NASB; cf. Mark 9:33–34). Jesus responded to their prideful quarrel by saying one must radically change and "become like children" (Matt 18:3 NASB) to enter heaven. What did he mean? The humility in verse 4 to make a commitment to Christ is likely the new

---

his spiritual gift that came about from a meeting with elders (4:14), and (3) the command to kindle afresh his spiritual gift (2 Tim 1:6).

change he meant.[45] This humble person will be the greatest in the kingdom of heaven (v. 4). Then Jesus used step parallelism: (1) when you receive a child, (2) you receive Jesus, and (3) you also receive the Father (Mark 9:37; Luke 9:48).[46]

Positive Metaphors

There is much use of "children" and "sons" as useful metaphors in the NT. John used "little children" as a term of endearment for his letter recipients in 1–3 John (e.g., 1 John 2:1; 2 John 1:1, 4; 3 John 1:4). A new Christian was a child in the faith and needed appropriate nourishment (1 Cor 3:1–2; Heb 5:12–13). At times, "children" is used as a positive label for a group of followers, such as in the verse, "Wisdom is vindicated by all her children" (Luke 7:35 NASB). Similarly, Jesus's followers are "sons of God" (Matt 5:9 NASB), "sons of your Father" (v. 45 NASB), "sons of the Most High" (Luke 6:35 NASB), "sons of the kingdom" (Matt 8:12; 13:38 NASB), "sons of the resurrection" (Luke 20:36 NASB), "sons of light" (Luke 16:8 NASB; cf. John 12:36), "sons of day" (1 Thess 5:5 NASB),[47] and "children of God" (1 John 3:2 NASB). Additionally, a common Semitic idiom was to emphasize a characteristic in someone by calling him a "son of" that quality. The expression could be positive, such as the nickname Barnabas, meaning "Son of Encouragement" (Acts 4:36 NASB). Jesus's favorite self-designation was "Son of Man," a messianic term

---

[45] France, *Matthew*, 677–79.

[46] Matthew shortened the step parallelism in 18:5 by omitting the last element.

[47] In these uses, "sons" is generic for "children."

that emphasized his humanity.[48] He used "little ones" to refer to new believers in him (Matt 18:6, 10, 14 NASB).

Luke 14:26, on the surface, looks dangerous to children; however, it contains a Hebraism and is problematic only if one misunderstands it. Jesus did not tell people literally to hate their parents, spouse, siblings, and children, because that would contradict his calls to love others (Matt 5:43–46; John 13:34–35; 15:17). Rather, there were two important choices, the love of God and love of family. Love of God must come first and is the more important choice, and "hate" represents the other choice.[49] Matthew omits this Hebraism and says not to love family more than God (v. 10:37).

Negative Examples and Metaphors

The NT contains some negative examples of children. When Jesus sent out the Twelve for ministry, he warned them about future persecution, saying that it will become so bad that families will be turned upside down. "Children will rise up against parents and cause them to be put to death" (Matt 10:21 NASB).[50] Later, Jesus likened the unbelieving generation who rejected him and John the Baptist to mean children in the streets who criticized those who did not play with them (Matt 11:16–19; Luke 7:31–35).

---

[48] "Son of Man" occurs 107 times in the OT. It occurs 88 times in the NT, 84 times as a self-reference by Jesus. The messianic term "Son of David" is used for Jesus 13 times in the NT.

[49] Edwards, *Luke*, 426.

[50] Mark records Jesus also giving this description in the Passion Week during his account of the Olivet Discourse, which some scholars call the Little Apocalypse (Mark 13:12).

Childishness is a negative metaphor. Acting like a child is expected of children (1 Cor 13:11); however, when a mature person acts as a child, this is a problem. Paul told the Christians at Corinth they should be mature Christians who ate solid spiritual food. Instead, they were still "babes in Christ" (*nēpiois en Christō*, 1 Cor 3:1, author's own translation) who still needed milk (v. 2). Similarly, the recipients of the letter to the Hebrews already should have been spiritual teachers, but each one was a "babe" (*nēpios*) who still needed milk and not solid food (Heb 5:12–14).

There are fewer negative "son of" metaphors in the NT than positive ones. Nonbelievers are "sons of this age" (Luke 16:8; 20:34 NASB), "sons of disobedience" (Eph 2:2 NASB), and "children of the devil" (1 John 3:10 NASB). Similarly, there are some negative Semitisms. Jesus gave the hotheads James and John the nickname Boanerges, meaning "Sons of Thunder" (Mark 3:17). Paul called Elymas "you son of the devil" (Acts 13:10 NASB). The Antichrist is the "son of destruction" (2 Thess 2:3).

Conclusion

Similar to the way OT teachings about children differed greatly from pagan teachings of the day, NT teachings about them differed from the perspective of the Greco-Roman world. The NT affirms the value of children. Not only do they help their individual families, but they also have worth and respective roles. More importantly, they can join God's kingdom through faith in Christ, participate in his plans, and grow in spiritual maturity. Jesus affirmed the value of children by receiving them, blessing them, loving them, healing them, and using them as object lessons to show their value. Jesus used them as both positive and negative spiritual examples, as does the rest of the NT.

Discussion Questions

1. What positive qualities of a child in the NT can I emulate in my walk with Christ?
2. How does the NT perspective on children differ from current society's perspective? How can I apply the NT teachings in my life and teach it to other people?
3. How does God use children in his plans today?
4. How can I teach children at home like Eunice and Lois and in church ministry like Paul?

Opportunities for Application

- When your church's Bible study or small group curriculum includes accounts of family life, add in discussion questions to help adults contemplate their valuation of children compared to the NT views noted in this chapter.

- Evaluate your church's inclusion of children in congregational events. Plan three or four new ways to affirm the worth and role of children in your church.

- Consider providing parenting courses or seminars a few times each year for parents in various stages of life—for example, new parents, parents of preschoolers, parents of children and/or preteens. Seminars could address the needs of many parents such as (1) understanding the spiritual development of children and how parents can best nurture their children, (2) strengthening their personal spiritual discipline practices, and (3) discipling children. In what other areas do parents in your church need support?

CHAPTER 3

Baptist Beliefs on Original Sin, the Age of Accountability, and Infant Salvation[1]

Adam Harwood

[1] An earlier version of this chapter was presented at a regional meeting of the Evangelical Theological Society at Southwestern Baptist Theological Seminary, Fort Worth, Texas, March 25, 2023. Thanks to my colleague Donna Peavey, who provided me with opportunities in the last ten years to speak to students in her children's ministry graduate courses at New Orleans Baptist Theological Seminary. Engaging with her students has aided in refining my thinking and clarifying my writing on theological issues concerning infants and children. Thanks also to Matt James, a colleague who provided constructive feedback on this chapter.

Introduction

Mark 10 records this encounter between Jesus and young children,

> People were bringing little children to him in order that he might touch them, but the disciples rebuked them. When Jesus saw it, he was indignant and said to them, "Let the little children come to me. Don't stop them, because the kingdom of God belongs to such as these. Truly I tell you, whoever does not receive the kingdom of God like a little child will never enter it." After taking them in his arms, he laid his hands on them and blessed them. (vv. 13–16)

Notice that Jesus's disciples attempted to keep people from bringing "little children" (Greek, *paidia*) to Jesus for a blessing. His disciples attempted to send them away. In response, Jesus was "indignant" and welcomed them. "Don't stop them," Jesus explained, "because the kingdom of God belongs to such as these" (see also the parallel accounts in Matt 19:13–15 and Luke 18:15–17). Jesus pointed to the young children as examples to the adults of how one should receive God's kingdom. Jesus then took the young children in his arms and laid his hands on them—according to the original request of those who brought the children—and Jesus blessed them. What are the implications for Baptist theology and ministry of Jesus welcoming and blessing young children? Some Christian traditions point to this episode to justify infant baptism, but Baptists do not practice infant baptism. If infants do not need to be baptized, then do Baptists regard them as sinners? Are infants and young children accountable to God? How do Baptists think God treats those people who, tragically, die in infancy?

There is no *single* Baptist belief about the spiritual condition of infants and young children. Nevertheless, a range of widely affirmed views on the subject can be gleaned from historic Baptist confessions and the writings of their theologians. This chapter will present views generally affirmed by most Baptists—today and historically—on three topics concerning the spiritual condition of infants and young children: original sin, the age of accountability, and infant salvation. Key biblical texts, interpretations, and theological positions for each area will be noted. This chapter will build on previous work on the topic and is intended to be a resource on Baptist perspectives on infants and children in Scripture, church history, and ministry.

Original Sin

Original sin is the idea that all people are sinners due to Adam and Eve's sin in the garden. Historic confessions of faith from every Christian tradition affirm human sin, the need for redemption provided by Christ's incarnation, and the atonement accomplished through his death and resurrection. Even so, the precise relationship between Adam's sin and subsequent generations of human sin and condemnation is unclear. How exactly does Adam's sin impact us today? In his book on the doctrine of sin, Tom McCall (a Wesleyan theologian) identifies six categories for classifying Christian views of the relationship between Adam's sin and subsequent generations of human sin and guilt.[2] McCall's categories are

[2] See the categories, definitions, and analysis of historic Christian theories of original sin in Thomas H. McCall, *Against God and Nature: The Doctrine of Sin*, Foundations of Evangelical Theology (Crossway, 2019), 149–76. See also my adoption and adaptation of those categories in Adam Harwood, *Christian Theology: Biblical, Historical, and Systematic* (Lexham Academic, 2022), 353–85.

1. symbolic and existential interpretations,
2. corruption-only,
3. federalism,
4. realism,
5. mediate views, and
6. conditional imputation of guilt.

These are helpful and nuanced categories. When considering Baptist views of original sin, I will set aside the first category, because I am unaware of any historic Baptist confession that interprets Adam as only symbolic and disregards his existence as a historical person. The second view, which I have renamed "inherited consequences," is a major view among Baptists. Inherited consequences is the understanding that all people inherit the *consequences* of Adam's sin, such as a corrupt nature, mortality, and a fallen world; however, people become guilty and fall under God's condemnation due to their own sin alone.[3] Views 3–6 are all versions of the other perspective found among Baptists, which I have categorized under the term "inherited guilt." Inherited guilt is the view that as a result of Adam's sin, all people inherit a corrupt nature, mortality, a fallen world, *and guilt*.[4] What are the key biblical texts and Baptist interpretations of those verses on original sin?

Key biblical texts on original sin include Rom 5:12; 1 Cor 15:22; Eph 2:3; and Ps 51:5. Romans 5:12 is the most significant text when discussing original sin.[5] The verse states, "Therefore, just as through

---

[3] Harwood, 374.

[4] Harwood, 369.

[5] As evidence for this claim, Rick Brannan, content innovation manager at Faithlife (the publisher of Logos Bible Software), explained that Bible passages from more than three hundred systematic theology titles had been categorized in a database according to classic doctrinal categories. Under the

one man sin entered into the world, and death through sin, and so death spread to all men, because all sinned" (NASB 1995). First Corinthians 15:22 is another prominent text cited in discussions of original sin. The verse states, "For as in Adam all die, so also in Christ all will be made alive" (NASB 1995). Also, Paul writes in Eph 2:3, "Among them we too all formerly lived in the lusts of our flesh, indulging the desires of the flesh and of the mind, and were by nature children of wrath, even as the rest" (NASB 1995). And David prays in Ps 51:5, "Behold, I was brought forth in iniquity / And in sin my mother conceived me" (NASB 1995). Though other passages could be cited, these are the verses most frequently noted when theologians and confessions refer to human sin and our connection to the original sinner.

Inherited Guilt

Some Baptists interpret the verses above with a theological pre-understanding that all humans share in both the corruption and guilt of Adam. Anabaptist Balthasar Hubmaier (1480–1528) argued a lengthy case from Scripture against infant baptism.[6] In 1527, Hubmaier published a document in response to a reply by

---

doctrine of sin, Rom 5:12 was referred to more than any other verse—more than twice as frequently as the second most common verse, Eph 2:3. Rick Brannan, "Writing a Systematic Theology? Top 100 Bible References to Cover," June 5, 2017, https://www.logos.com/grow/writing-systematic-theology/.

[6] Anthony L. Chute et al., *The Baptist Story: From English Sect to Global Movement* (B&H Academic, 2015), affirm the "spiritual kinship" that modern Baptists have to many Anabaptists due to similar views of regenerate church membership, believer's baptism, congregational polity, and church-state separation (5). For that reason, I am including an Anabaptist as a representative among Baptists.

Oecolampadius addressing an in-person dialogue between Anabaptist and Swiss Reformed pastors in his home in 1525. Hubmaier quotes Oecolampadius as stating that children "are without all sin and are unspotted."[7] Hubmaier's reply begins, "If the children are without sin and unspotted why would Job and Jeremiah curse the day of their birth, Job 3:3; Jer. 20:14f? Why does David complain that he was conceived in sin and that his mother gave birth to him in evil, Ps. 51:5? Why does Paul testify that we are all by nature children of wrath, Eph. 2:3, and all have sinned in Adam, 1 Cor. 15:22?"[8] Hubmaier accuses Oecolampadius of following Zwingli by arguing for the error of "godless infant baptism."[9] Hubmaier then explains that Oecolampadius was punished by God and so fell into another error, teaching that "original sin is no sin."[10] In this document and others, Hubmaier indicates that infants are sinners by nature and in Adam. Hubmaier's teaching that all people sin *in Adam*, as well as his rejection of Zwingli's view of original sin as "disease" (corruption) rather than "sin" (which implies guilt), position Hubmaier's view under the category of inherited guilt.

The Southern Baptist Theological Seminary's founder, first president, and theology professor, James P. Boyce (1827–1888), followed Presbyterian theologian Charles Hodge in approaching the

---

[7] Balthasar Hubmaier, *On Infant Baptist Against Oecolampad*, in *Balthasar Hubmaier: Theologian of Anabaptism*, trans. and ed. H. Wayne Pipkin and John H. Yoder, Classics of the Radical Reformation 5 (1989), 284. Note 38 indicates that Oecolampadius said "own sin," not "all sin." Though Hubmaier might have wrongly accused Oecolampadius of denying original sin, the relevant issue is Hubmaier's view of original sin.

[8] Hubmaier, *On Infant Baptist Against Oecolampad*, 284. The question marks are periods in the original.

[9] Hubmaier, 285.

[10] Hubmaier, 285.

biblical texts on original sin by presupposing the theological framework known as the covenant of works.[11] The covenant of works, as defined by the Westminster Confession of Faith (1647), is the understanding that God promised Adam and his descendants life if he obeyed but judgment on Adam and his descendants if he disobeyed.[12] In that way, Adam was the "head" of humanity. Boyce dedicated an entire chapter to describing the headship of Adam.[13] He explained that God "regards a sinful nature as deserving punishment equally with a sinful act," and people "may be punished for the corrupt nature thus inherited, although they may not have been personally guilty of a single transgression."[14] In this way, "guilt was incurred through Adam."[15] Like Hubmaier, Boyce affirmed that all humanity sinned in Adam. Boyce wrote, "The mass of mankind proceeding from Adam by natural generation sinned in him, not consciously, but representatively."[16]

The Baptist Faith and Message (BFM) of 1925 states that Adam's "posterity inherit a nature corrupt and in bondage to sin,

---

[11] For the influence of Charles Hodge on James P. Boyce, see Ernest Reisinger and Fred Malone, "Introduction to 1977 edition," in James P. Boyce, *Abstract of Systematic Theology* (Founders, 2006), v, who note that Boyce used Hodge's systematic text at The Southern Baptist Theological Seminary for a period of time. Also, see the citation of Hodge's *Outline of Theology* in Boyce, 235, when Hodge explained the covenant of works.

[12] James Leo Garrett Jr., *Baptist Theology: A Four-Century Study* (Mercer University Press, 2009), notes, "Among the confessions of faith produced by the magisterial wing of the Reformation the mid-seventeenth century Westminster Confession of Faith (1647) was by far the most influential on early Baptist confessions of faith" (7).

[13] Boyce, *Abstract of Systematic Theology*, 247–58.

[14] Boyce, 250.

[15] Boyce, 256.

[16] Boyce, 251.

are under condemnation, and as soon as they are capable of moral action, become actual transgressors."[17] The theology of BFM 1925 fits under the category of inherited guilt because the confessional statement places condemnation *before* moral action and actual transgression, which implies condemnation of individuals due to their inherited corrupt nature.

Hubmaier, Boyce, and the BFM 1925 represent Baptists who affirm an understanding of original sin called inherited guilt.

Inherited Consequences

Inherited consequences is the other major view of original sin among Baptist theologians, confessions, and members in the pews. According to this perspective, most of what was affirmed in the previous view is also believed. According to the inherited consequences view, all people inherit the consequences of Adam's sin, such as a corrupt nature, mortality, and a fallen world; however, people *become* guilty and fall under God's condemnation due to their *own sin alone*. All humans are negatively impacted by Adam's sin and will—granting the conditions of natural mental and moral development—attain moral capability, knowingly sin, and are accountable to God for knowing the difference between right and wrong yet choosing to do wrong.

The key biblical texts interpreted to support the previous view of original sin are interpreted by others to support the view known as inherited consequences. Romans 5:12 is interpreted to mean

[17] "Comparison of 1925, 1963, and 2000 Baptist Faith and Message," in *Baptist Faith and Message 2000: Critical Issues in America's Largest Protestant Denomination*, ed. Douglas K. Blount and Joseph D. Wooddell (Rowman & Littlefield, 2007), 206.

that sin entered the world through Adam's sin. Neither Rom 5:12 nor 1 Cor 15:22 state that subsequent generations of people sin *in Adam*. Rather, all people will die "because all sinned" (Rom 5:12 NASB 1995). Also, the context of 1 Cor 15 concerns *physical* death and *bodily* resurrection. Thus, the phrase in verse 22, "in Adam all die" (NASB 1995), refers to all people *dying physically* as Adam died, not to all people being guilty due to Adam's sin. In parallel, the phrase "in Christ all will be made alive" (NASB 1995) refers to the *bodily raising* of all the dead by Christ on the day of judgment (1 Cor 15:22; see also Dan 12:2 and John 5:28–29). The "by nature children of wrath" phrase in Eph 2:3 (NASB 1995) indicates that people who are *unbelievers* are subject to God's wrath due to their *sinful acts*, not due to a condemned status at the time of their physical birth. Also, David's comments in Ps 51:5 about being sinful at birth and conceived in sin are widely understood as lamenting the pervasiveness of his sin, which reached the earliest moments of his life. David was not indicting either his conception or himself as an infant as guilty of sin.[18]

In "A Short Confession of Faith in Twenty Articles," English General Baptist John Smyth (1570–1612) wrote, "There is no original sin (lit., no sin of origin or descent), but all sin is actual and voluntary, viz., a word, a deed, or a design against the law of God; and therefore, infants are without sin."[19]

---

[18] For more on Augustine's influential interpretations of these and other verses on original sin, as well as counter-interpretations of the verses, see Harwood, *Christian Theology*, 358–66.

[19] See "A Short Confession of Faith in Twenty Articles by John Smyth," in *Baptist Confessions of Faith*, ed. William L. Lumpkin (Judson, 1978), 100–101.

Baptist statesman E. Y. Mullins (1860–1928) also rejected the doctrine of inherited guilt.[20] He explained that a man "is guilty when he does wrong."[21] Mullins clarified, "Men are not condemned therefore for hereditary or original sin. They are condemned only for their own sins."[22]

W. T. Conner (1877–1952), theology professor at Southwestern Baptist Theological Seminary (SWBTS) from 1910–1949, rejected inherited guilt. Conner taught that sin implies willful disobedience to God, which requires the knowledge of moral truth. Sin is universal, inevitable, and hereditary due to our relationship with Adam. Nevertheless, Conner explained, "The idea that Adam's sin as an act of sin is charged to his descendants and on that account they are guilty and hence condemned, is an idea too preposterous to be seriously entertained."[23]

In his systematic theology, Canadian Baptist Stanley J. Grenz (1950–2005) wrote, "Romans 5:12–21, like Ephesians 2:3, does not clearly and unequivocally declare that all persons inherit guilt directly because of Adam's sin. The biblical case for original guilt is not strong." Grenz concluded, "Our human nature has been corrupted."[24]

James Leo Garrett Jr. (1925–2020) provided a historical perspective: "Southern Seminary has had a wide divergence of views on your

---

[20] In addition to serving as a pastor and theology professor, E. Y. Mullins served in the previous century as president of The Southern Baptist Theological Seminary, the Southern Baptist Convention, and the Baptist World Alliance.

[21] E. Y. Mullins, *The Christian Religion in Its Doctrinal Expression* (Sunday School Board, 1917), 294.

[22] Mullins, 302.

[23] W. T. Conner, *The Gospel of Redemption* (Broadman, 1945), 29.

[24] Stanley J. Grenz, *Theology for the Community of God* (Eerdmans, 2000), 205.

topic [of original sin]; for example, between Boyce and Dale Moody and between Dale Moody and Al Mohler. Southwestern Seminary, on the other hand, has consistently been on one side: we are not guilty of Adam's sin. Walter T. Conner repeatedly took this stance." Garrett explained that for more than one century, the theology faculty at SWBTS affirmed unanimously that people are not guilty of Adam's sin. Garrett explained, "Conner was the theology department at SWBTS from 1910 to 1949. I have known, I believe, every person who has taught theology as a full faculty member since 1949, and I cannot identify any one of these who taught that we are all guilty of the sin of Adam (and Eve), with one possible exception."[25] According to Garrett, various generations of the faculty of Southern Seminary have differed on the view of inherited guilt, but the faculty of SWBTS has always rejected it. Though Garrett does not identify himself as rejecting inherited guilt, this is a reasonable inference, because he taught theology at SWBTS during the second half of the previous century and thus would be counted among the theology faculty that he claims rejected the view.

The 1963 and 2000 revisions of the BFM are consistent with the inherited consequences view. The 1963 and 2000 versions of article 3 are identical in this section of the article titled "Man." According to the BFM, Adam's "posterity inherit a nature and an environment inclined toward sin. Therefore, as soon as they are capable of moral action, they become transgressors and are under condemnation."[26] The

[25] The one possible exception was a new faculty member whose view on original sin Garrett did not know. James Leo Garrett Jr., correspondence to the author, January 22, 2013, used with permission.

[26] "Comparison of 1925, 1963, and 2000 Baptist Faith and Message," 206. The 2000 version added the words "Therefore" and "they" and smoothed out the punctuation, but the substance of the article was unchanged.

article affirms an inherited human *inclination* to commit sinful actions, but the BFM does not claim that people inherit Adam's guilt and condemnation. Herschel Hobbs explained that the 1963 revision of the article on man "agrees with the position generally held by Baptists concerning God's grace in cases of those under the age of accountability and the mentally incompetent."[27] Hobbs explained that the change made in 1963 to article 3 was intended to reflect the commonly held view that God provides grace for those under the age of accountability and those individuals who are mentally incompetent. That 1963 revision to article 3 was unchanged during the 2000 revision to the BFM and remains unchanged at the time of the writing of this chapter.

Smyth, Mullins, Conner, Grenz, Garrett, and the 1963 and 2000 versions of the BFM represent Baptists who affirm an understanding of original sin called inherited consequences.

Two Views of Original Sin

Though Baptists affirm two views of original sin, inherited guilt and inherited consequences, both views are orthodox (meaning faithful, permissible, and defensible) viewpoints. Both views affirm the devastating impact of Adam's sin on humanity, humanity's broken relationship with God, and the need for God's gracious acts in Christ's incarnation, cross, and resurrection to restore us to himself. Also, both views of original sin can be found in major historic confessions and the writings of faithful Christian teachers in both the Baptist tradition and the wider Christian community.

---

[27] Herschel H. Hobbs, "Southern Baptists and Confessionalism: A Comparison of the Origins and Contents of the 1925 and 1963 Confessions," *Review and Expositor* 76.1 (1979): 63.

The Age of Accountability

The age of accountability is the view that God does not hold infants and young children accountable for the sinful thoughts, attitudes, and actions for which God holds older people accountable. This concept has been affirmed widely by Baptists; despite its name, the view does not focus on a chronological age. The idea is not that children become accountable to God at a particular age, such as their thirteenth birthday. Rather, the idea is that infants and children are not yet accountable to God until they reach an age or stage of moral accountability. How to pinpoint that age or stage is unknown. Nevertheless, one can affirm the concept as helpful for explaining the human condition without attempting to explain how God deals with the various situations posed by each person's mental and moral development. However, some Christian theologians have questioned whether the age of accountability can be supported by Scripture.[28] Those who affirm the concept point to several biblical texts that they believe imply that God does not hold infants and young children accountable for sin in the same way God holds morally competent people accountable for sin.

Biblical texts cited to support an age of accountability include Deut 1:39; Isa 7:15–16; Jonah 4:11; Romans 1–2; and Rom 7:9. In Deut 1:39, the Israelite children were not held responsible for the

---

[28] See, for example, Wayne Grudem, *Systematic Theology: An Introduction to Biblical Doctrine* (Zondervan, 1994), who writes, "Some maintain that Scripture teaches an 'age of accountability' before which young children are not held responsible for sin and are not counted guilty before God. However, the passages noted above in Section C about 'inherited sin' indicate that even before birth children have a guilty standing before God and a sinful nature that not only gives them a tendency to sin but also causes God to view them as 'sinners'" (499).

sinful actions of the older generations in the desert. Isaiah 7:15–16 and Jonah 4:11 refer to a period when people do not yet know the difference between good and evil, right and wrong. According to Romans 1–2, God's judgment seems to be in response to sinful acts of people who know the truth. God judges people as idolaters and lawbreakers because they know there is a God and universal law, yet they worship created things and break God's law. If God's judgment of humans includes his assessment of their actions and knowledge, then infants and young children would be excluded. Also, Paul writes in Rom 7:9, "I was once alive apart from the Law; but when the commandment came, sin became alive and I died" (NASB 1995). Paul's statement could be understood to mean that he was spiritually alive early in life and then died spiritually due to his disobedience to God's commands before he was made alive spiritually through union with Christ. According to this interpretation, Paul described himself as spiritually alive as an infant and young child before he attained moral accountability, knowingly sinned, and died spiritually.

W. T. Conner explained that "seeds of evil tendency in the child's nature" will eventually result in the child committing an act of transgression upon reaching an "age of moral responsibility." Before that time, though, the child "does not have personal guilt" because he or she has not yet developed personal responsibility, namely, "the powers of self-consciousness and self-determination."[29] Conner used the phrase "age of moral responsibility" when he described what we have referred to as an age of accountability.

Stanley J. Grenz referred to the age of accountability when he described the development of human moral responsibility. He

---

[29] W. T. Conner, *Christian Doctrine* (Broadman, 1937), 143.

explained, "Somewhere in childhood we move from a stage in which our actions are not deemed morally accountable to the responsibility of acting as moral agents. In short, we cross a point which some refer to as the 'age of accountability.'"[30]

Millard J. Erickson (b. 1932) explains his view of the age of accountability in his systematic theology textbook. He believes that all people begin life as participants in the sin and guilt of Adam. However, Erickson also argues for a conditional imputation of guilt. He explains that the Lord excludes "infants and those who never reach moral competence" from condemnation. He cites Matt 19:14 and 2 Sam 12:23 to support his position, and he concludes that people are "not morally responsible before a certain point, which we sometimes call 'the age of accountability.'" Erickson affirms a conditional imputation of Adam's guilt with "no condemnation until one reaches the age of responsibility." At that point, when we become aware of our "tendency toward sin" and decide to commit a sinful action due to our sinful nature, then our "childish innocence" ends. He explains, "We become responsible and guilty when we accept or approve of our corrupt nature." At that point, we ratify the work of Adam in our own lives, and Adam's guilt is imputed to us.[31]

James Leo Garrett Jr. observed that "the New Testament is silent as to the spiritual state or condition of infants or young children before God." Even so, Garrett wrote, "The question as to the time (or times) when human beings first come to the consciousness of sin leads to the theological topic which Baptists and other adherents

---

[30] Grenz, *Theology for the Community of God*, 209.

[31] Millard J. Erickson, *Christian Theology*, 3rd ed. (Baker, 2013), 581–82.

to believer's baptism only have called 'the age of accountability,' or 'the age of discretion.' Such an age has been normally understood or defined as the time when one may attain to a true and responsible consciousness of sin." He noted that some call this "the age of respondability."[32]

Billy Graham (1918–2018), a Baptist evangelist who proclaimed the gospel to tens of millions of people, commented on original sin in one of his books. In Graham's view, Adam and Eve sinned by choice, and subsequent generations inherit "the tendency to sin" and become "sinners by choice" due to their sin and rebellion against God upon reaching the age of accountability.[33]

According to the 1963 and 2000 revisions of the BFM, Adam's "posterity inherit a nature and an environment inclined toward sin. Therefore, as soon as they are capable of moral action, they become transgressors and are under condemnation." One may reasonably infer from these statements in the BFM that infants and young children have not yet reached an age or stage of moral accountability before God, will *later* become capable of moral actions, and will certainly transgress God's laws and then fall under God's just condemnation. Until they attain moral accountability, however, they are safe from God's condemnation.

Conner, Grenz, Erickson, Garrett, Graham, and the 1963 and 2000 revisions of the BFM represent Baptist views on the age of accountability.

---

[32] James Leo Garrett Jr., *Systematic Theology: Biblical, Historical, and Evangelical*, vol. 1, 4th ed. (Wipf & Stock, 2014), 580–81.

[33] Billy Graham, *World Aflame* (Doubleday, 1965), 71. See also Howell Walker Burkhead, "The Development of the Concept of Sin in the Preaching of Billy Graham" (PhD diss., SWBTS, 1998), 106.

Infant Salvation

Though Baptists affirm two major views of original sin—inherited guilt and inherited consequences—they affirm one view of infant salvation. With rare exceptions, Baptists believe and teach that all who die as infants and young children are safe with God, not held accountable by God for their inclination toward sin, and welcomed by God into heaven by God's grace through Christ's work on the cross.

Biblical texts sometimes noted in discussions of infant salvation include David mourning his son and Jesus welcoming the children. In the former text, David declared that he would one day see his deceased infant son (2 Sam 12:23). Because David stated that he would one day see his son and also believed that he would be with the Lord after his own death (Ps 16:10–11), it is reasonable to infer that David believed his deceased son was with the Lord. In the Gospel text, Jesus held up infants and children as examples of people to whom the kingdom of heaven belongs (Matt 19:14; see also Mark 10:14 and Luke 18:16). Though Jesus did not refer explicitly to salvation, he neither condemned the infants and children nor commanded them to repent. Instead, Jesus welcomed them, blessed them, and pointed to them as examples of kingdom citizens.

The same two representatives for inherited guilt also argued for the salvation of all who die in infancy. When addressing the eternal destiny of unbaptized infants, Balthasar Hubmaier implied that if God were to exercise only his justice, then those who die in infancy would remain in their sin. Nevertheless, God—who exercises mercy on some people—can be trusted to be merciful. Hubmaier acknowledged that Scripture is not clear on the matter of infant salvation. Even so, he seemed to make the case that infants (who are unable to exercise faith) can be saved by God's grace apart from their parents' faith, infant faith, or infant baptism.[34]

Though James Boyce affirmed views consistent with inherited guilt, he also taught that regeneration may occur without faith and conversion, specifically citing infants.[35] Also, Boyce quoted approvingly from A. A. Hodge, who concluded that through an application of the atonement, "All dying in infancy are redeemed and saved."[36]

E. Y. Mullins admitted that "there is comparatively little direct teaching in the Scriptures as to the salvation of infants dying in infancy."[37] Nevertheless, "Christ's union with the human race made his atoning work efficacious in some measure for all mankind." Quoting 1 Cor 15:22, he rejected Universalism (the view that all people will be saved) but suggested a "similarity" between the effects of the acts of Adam and those of the acts of Christ for humanity. People will be condemned for rejecting Christ's work on their behalf. Mullins reasoned, "Infants dying in infancy cannot repent, or believe, or perform works of any kind, good or bad. We do not know how the grace of God operates in them. But we are fully assured that Christ provided for them, and that they are created anew in him and saved."[38]

William Wilson Stevens (1914–1978), professor of Bible and New Testament at Mississippi College, addressed the topic of infant salvation in his book, *Doctrines of the Christian Religion*. Though acknowledging that the Scriptures provide little explicit teaching on

---

[34] Balthasar Hubmaier, *On the Christian Baptism of Believers*, in Pipkin and Yoder, *Balthasar Hubmaier*, 139–43.

[35] Boyce, *Abstract of Systematic Theology*, 381.

[36] Boyce, 338.

[37] Mullins, *The Christian Religion in Its Doctrinal Expression*, 301.

[38] Mullins, 302.

the topic, Stevens stated that "they heavily imply that an infant who dies is saved." He explained, "Since infants cannot repent, or believe, or perform works that are good or bad, we do not understand how the grace of God in Christ operates for their benefit. Yet we know that Christ provided for them and that his redeeming power is effective in them."[39]

Robert P. Lightner (1931–2018) taught Bible and theology courses at Baptist Bible Seminary and Dallas Theological Seminary for almost fifty years. He published a popular-level book titled *Safe in the Arms of Jesus: God's Provision for the Death of Those Who Cannot Believe*. Lightner wrote, "In all of the Bible references to infants and young children, not once is there so much as a hint that they will ever be eternally lost and separated from God if they die before they have had an opportunity to respond to the gospel."[40] After noting the absence of commands in the Scripture for them to repent, Lightner notes that Adam "represented the whole human race." His disobedience affected every person. Nevertheless, Jesus Christ's death and resurrection "paid the debt brought about by sin for everyone, the same group affected by the first Adam's sin." Those who refuse to repent and believe in Jesus as their Savior will not go to heaven. However, "all of those who have never been able to understand" will go to heaven when they die. All people "are born in a state of condemnation."[41] However, unbelieving adults and unable-to-believe infants and young children are in different spiritual conditions. The sin debt of infants was paid in full by Christ at the cross, and "the

---

[39] William Wilson Stevens, *Doctrines of the Christian Religion* (Eerdmans, 1967), 162–63.

[40] Robert P. Lightner, *Safe in the Arms of Jesus: God's Provision for the Death of Those Who Cannot Believe* (Kregel, 2000), 15.

[41] Lightner, 23–24.

debt is canceled until it is rejected. Therefore, God can receive into His presence all those who did not receive His Son by faith because they *could not* do so."[42]

Hubmaier, Boyce, Mullins, Stevens, and Lightner represent Baptist views on infant salvation. The consensus is that God, by his grace and through Christ's work on the cross, welcomes all who die in infancy into heaven.

Objection to This View and a Brief Reply

Someone might object: If God saves all who die in infancy, then does this view justify abortion or infanticide? In reply, no. God forbids taking an innocent human life (Gen 9:6). The result that God would welcome the innocent victim into heaven does not justify the immoral and sinful act of taking the innocent life. Also, the case for infant salvation is inferred from Scripture, but the prohibition against taking an innocent human life is explicit. Further, God is clear that he desires believers to make disciples (Matt 28:18–20) and produce a godly heritage (Mal 2:15). Thus, God desires to populate heaven by faithful evangelism, discipleship, and godly parenting—not by the slaughter of the innocent.

Conclusion

As we have seen, there is no *single* Baptist belief about the spiritual condition of infants and young children. However, the sampling of Baptist confessions and theologians in this chapter points toward

---

[42] Lightner, *Safe*, 24–25, emphasis his.

the views generally affirmed by most Baptists on original sin, the age of accountability, and infant salvation. Baptists affirm Scripture's statements that the consequences of Adam's sin were devastating for humanity. Though we differ on whether infants and young children are under God's condemnation for sin, Baptists are united in affirming that God acted in Christ to rescue sinners. Many Baptists teach that infants and young children *become* accountable to God for their own sin. The consensus is that people who die as infants or young children are welcomed by God into heaven by God's grace and through Christ's work on the cross. Finally, Baptists seek to follow Jesus by welcoming little children and pointing to them as citizens of God's kingdom.

Discussion Questions

1. Which view of original sin do you affirm and why?
2. Do you find the case for the age of accountability to be persuasive? Why or why not?
3. How does your view of the age of accountability relate to your previous view of original sin? Do those views comport well with one another, or do you notice inconsistencies?
4. Discuss a pastoral care situation or funeral you have observed for an infant or young child. What are some of the considerations that pastors and children's ministers should keep in mind? If you have not personally observed this situation, you may use your imagination to craft a scenario. (Tips: Be present for an appropriate length of time with those who are in crisis; pray with and for them; offer to address practical needs; do not try to explain why a family is suffering.)

Opportunities for Application

- Imagine a concerned parent of a three-year-old asks you about the condition of his child's eternity. Write out what Scriptures you could share with that parent to guide him or her to see a biblical approach to understanding the spiritual condition of children who have yet to reach moral accountability.
- Evaluate your church's preschool and children's Bible teaching curriculum for biblical accuracy and age-appropriate activities. Lifeway Christian Resources has several training videos and materials that follow the tenets of the BFM. Other curriculums and teaching products exist that you can measure against the teaching in the Bible to discover if your church's teaching materials assist your leaders in laying solid biblical foundations for preschoolers and children.
- If your church has a ministry for expectant or new parents, consider training the team members on the spiritual condition of infants as well as grief care to help minister to parents who experience a miscarriage or the death of a young child. Remember that important days like Mother's Day and Father's Day can be difficult for couples who desire to be parents but may have experienced miscarriages or infertility.

CHAPTER 4

Evangelism and Children

Karen Kennemur

Becoming a Christian is not a complicated process. In fact, it is a simple one. According to Rom 10:9, it requires a confession that Jesus is Lord and a belief that Jesus died on the cross and arose from the grave to save people from their sins. The Bible further states the good news of Jesus Christ is for all people. In Matt 28:19, Jesus commanded the disciples to go into the world and share the gospel with all nations. For this chapter, it is important to note that *all nations* includes not only all ethnicities but all ages and certainly includes children.

God values children. In Deuteronomy, he commanded parents to tell their children of God and his love. God spoke to Samuel when he was a young child (1 Sam 3:1–15), and God allowed Josiah to become king at eight years old. The only miracle recorded in all four Gospels involved the faith of a child who gave his lunch to Jesus to share with over five thousand people. Jesus affirmed his love for children in Luke 18:16 when he told his disciples to "let the little children come to me, and don't stop them, because the kingdom of God belongs to such as these." Christians are to love children and share the good news of Jesus Christ with them.

D. L. Moody, the famous evangelist of the 1800s, said, "If I could relive my life, I would devote my entire ministry to reaching children for God."[1] In 1953, Gaines Dobbins wrote, "The winning of the children to Christ is not incidental. It is today's supreme imperative. Boys and girls . . . constitute the most significant group in our changing culture."[2] Millie Kohn, a children's minister at the First Baptist Church of Dallas in the 1960s and 1970s, told a story about a short-lived time for children's worship at her church. The Sunday worship attendance had become so great that space was needed in the sanctuary. Dr. W. A. Criswell, the pastor, asked Millie to start a worship service for children in the chapel. This would allow for space in the sanctuary for more adults. At the end of two years, no children had become Christians during the services. Dr. Criswell and Millie decided to end the children's worship service. The salvation of children was more important than the extra space in the sanctuary.[3]

Early in my ministry when I was a children's minister in the Dallas-Fort Worth area, a set of parents in my church asked me to speak with their son, Daniel, who was in the first grade and

---

[1] D. L. Moody, "Associate of Ministry in Children and Family Ministry," Moody Bible Institute, accessed July 2024, https://www.moody.edu/academics/programs/associate-children-family-ministry/.

[2] Gaines Dobbins, *Winning the Children* (Broadman, 1953), 2.

[3] Karen Kennemur, "The Prioritization of Southern Baptist Programs for Children Determined by Pastors, Children's Ministers, and Parents" (PhD diss., SWBTS, 2008) ProQuest (3341161), 18.

curious about becoming a Christian. Daniel was from a family with a Christian heritage. His parents and grandparents were involved in their local churches. Daniel grew up immersed in Christianity. As we talked, I began to present the gospel to Daniel. He firmly answered my questions. I came to the point in the conversation when I asked Daniel if he would like to become a Christian. He said, "No." I was stunned for a few seconds. I began praying about what to do next with this young man who, by his own admission, was not ready. Then we turned the conversation to what he should do when he was ready. Daniel and I prayed. I spoke with his parents. He went on his way and returned the next year ready to commit his life to Christ.

I have thought of this experience many times since. Daniel knew about Christ. He had grown up around involved believers, but he knew he was not ready to begin his own faith journey. He did not articulate these words, but the Holy Spirit was obviously not moving in his life yet. What a brave young man! He made an important decision that day and then the most important decision the next year.

The Time to Tell Children of the Good News of Jesus

A good question to ask is, At what age do we tell children the gospel of Jesus Christ? I believe we begin before their births. Christian parents can pray over their unborn child, sing and listen to Christian music, listen to sermons, and converse with other Christians, all creating a Christian environment for the new infant. Hopefully, these practices continue throughout childhood. A young child who grows up in a healthy, Christian environment where the good news of Jesus is spoken learns about faith from an early age. Optimistically, this gives a child a clear path to following Christ when prompted by the Holy Spirit.

Lifeway, a Baptist publishing house, writes Bible curriculum for all ages, beginning with newborns. The curriculum is designed around the development of children. The wholistic approach considers the physical, cognitive, social-emotional, and spiritual characteristics of children. Two documents in particular are helpful to parents and teachers: *Ages and Stages* and *Bible Skills for Kids*.[4] These documents aid adults when teaching children. *Ages and Stages* provides information and answers questions that help children strengthen their understanding of what it means to have a relationship with God, and *Bible Skills for Kids* provides ways to teach children spiritual disciplines. Meeting children where they are in life as they are taught about the love of God is important.

The Understanding of a Child

For many years, ministers, pastors, and children's leaders have discussed the age of accountability, which is defined as the "time or period of life when one is aware enough of God to respond to him."[5] Is this a certain age? When is a child old enough to become a Christian? Eight years old? Ten years old? God created people as individuals, each a uniquely created person. No two children or adults are alike. Is age the right measure, or is it the level of one's understanding? What does a child need to clearly understand to make a decision to follow Christ? Eugene Chamberlain wrote, "We will continue to have churches filled with unregenerate church members. Regardless of the age at which children face this decision, they

---

[4] Lifeway Kids and Lifeway Students, *Ages and Stages* (Lifeway Christian Resources, 2021); Lifeway Kids, *Bible Skills for Kids* (Lifeway Christian Resources, 2017).

[5] Clifford Ingle, *Children and Conversion* (Broadman, 1970), 84.

deserve sound guidance. If more children are to become Christians and church members at an earlier age, let them do so with better and better guidance from their parents and workers."[6] This debate will most likely continue. However, most children's ministers consider the level of understanding with the Holy Spirit's prompting rather than a chronological age as the mark of readiness.

If understanding is the marker, what are the points that need to be understood to be a follower of Christ? The training manual developed by the North American Mission Board, *Sharing God's Special Plan with Children,* suggests that the following points need to be understood for someone to become a Christian:[7]

1. A child must comprehend the concept of sin. Early in a child's life, parents begin teaching what is right and wrong. Toddlers are taught what they can touch and what they cannot. Preschoolers learn how to be kind to others. By the elementary years, most children understand how to follow rules and how to treat other people. Children may not label wrongdoing as sin, but most understand the concept of sin. Having significant adults in their lives can help them understand that sin is "actions, attitudes, words, or thoughts that do not please God."[8]
2. A child must understand that he or she is a sinner. For younger children, this is hard to grasp. They perceive themselves as good people and believe good people are not sinners.

---

[6] Eugene Chamberlain, *When Can a Child Believe?* (Broadman, 1973), 16–17.

[7] North American Mission Board, *Sharing God's Special Plan with Children* (North American Mission Board, 1993), 7–9.

[8] Landry R. Holmes and Judy H. Latham, eds., *Holman Illustrated Bible Dictionary for Kids* (B&H, 2010), 179.

Many young children see the sin of others before they see their own sin. For example, siblings easily point out the sins of their brothers or sisters, such as when a sibling steals a cookie from the kitchen or knocks over their block tower. Young children have a hard time fully comprehending their own sins, but only a sinner needs a Savior. Thus, it is vital that the child sees himself or herself as a sinner.

3. A child must recognize that his or her sin is against God. Hitting a sibling when a child is angry is not only a sin against a brother or sister, but it is also against God and his Word. Until a certain time of understanding, "a child will determine right and wrong on the basis of pain and pleasure."[9] However, sin is more than determining right and wrong, it is a sin against God. God uses the Holy Spirit to convict people of sin against God. As children grow and mature, they will begin to understand the prompting of the Holy Spirit. Samuel was young when he heard the voice of God. Samuel did not recognize the voice of God initially. Eli, a significant adult in Samuel's life, helped him understand that God was speaking to him. Thus, the understanding that sin not only hurts the sinner and other people but is also against God takes time and maturity to flourish in a child's life.
4. A child must realize sin separates a person from God. In the second and third chapters of Genesis, the writer shows how sin separates man from God. Adam and Eve lived in a beautiful garden and had a close relationship with God.

[9] North American Mission Board, *Sharing God's Special Plan with Children,* 8.

They had the perfect life until sin entered their world. Once the couple sinned, they were separated from God. "Then the man and his wife heard the sound of the LORD God walking in the garden at the time of the evening breeze, and they hid from the LORD" (Gen 3:8). Adam and Eve pulled away from God because of the shame of their sin. God sent them out of the garden to live a life of work and hardship. Sin separates people from God.

5. A child must comprehend the purpose of Jesus's death and resurrection, which was to save all people from the consequences of their sin. Without Jesus, people would be unforgiven sinners separated from God. Jesus took away the ultimate punishment for sin and made a path for people to have a personal relationship with God. Rom 6:23 says, "For the wages of sin is death, but the gift of God is eternal life in Christ Jesus our Lord." Jesus is the way to God.

Communication with Children

First, wording is important. If you have been a Christian for a long time, you may or may not realize that church people have a unique vocabulary. Church language consists of words and phrases like "holy," "salvation," "give your heart to Jesus," "saved," "lostness," and other terms. Churchy language has been coined as the "language of Zion." "The language [of Zion] consists of terms that adult Christians have used for generations. These terms have meaning to those who understand them but are often confusing to the uninitiated."[10] For example, if one says God is holy, a child may understand the term as "to be

[10] Chamberlain, *When Can a Child Believe?*, 56.

with holes." The child may respond with confusion and ask if God has holes in his clothing. Or, if a child is asked if she is lost, meaning without Christ, her response may be "no" because she knows her exact location. But the question was to determine whether she is a Christian. When talking to children about becoming a Christian, adults should use words a child understands.

Second, encourage children to express themselves with their own words and ideas. When discussing salvation with children, it is important for the child to express his or her own ideas using his or her words. The adult listens carefully to determine if the child has the level of understanding needed to make this life-altering decision. Once, when I was a children's minister, I was speaking with a first grader about becoming a Christian. She told me that she was covered in the blood of Jesus. Considering that most children at this age are concrete thinkers and not abstract thinkers, it did not appear that she was ready to become a Christian. As a concrete thinker, one does not want to be covered in anyone's blood! Plus, this particular little girl was an only child who lived with her Christian parents and Christian grandparents. It seemed to me that she was using the adult language that she often heard in her home. A year later, she did express her understanding in her own words. She then made a decision to follow Christ. Those who counsel children should always encourage children to express their thoughts in their own words. This helps children know for themselves that their decisions are real, and it helps the adult know if children truly understand the gospel.

Third, ask open-ended questions. Open-ended questions require more than a yes or no answer. They require a thoughtful answer. "Open-ended questions allow children to respond with more information about their understanding, attitudes, and feelings."[11] When speaking with a child who is showing interest in becoming a Christian, it is helpful to ask questions like the following: What is sin? Who is Jesus? Why did Jesus die on the cross? What is a Christian? Questions like these help the adult to understand the knowledge level of the child, and they help a child to know whether or not his or her understanding is correct.

Fourth, listen intently. Sometimes, when a child asks questions about becoming a Christian, the adult answering the child's questions becomes so excited that he or she takes over the conversation. Instead, the adult needs to listen intently, allowing the child to answer the questions, without the adult taking over the conversation with a lecture. The conversation should be mutually shared, with both persons speaking with ease.[12]

Fifth, never pressure a child. The day a child becomes a Christian is an exciting day for parents, children's leaders, pastors, and the church family. The thought of a person, especially a loved one, spending eternity in hell is heartbreaking to Christians. Christian parents rejoice the moment they know their child will spend eternity in heaven with Christ. But this excitement does not need to turn into pressure for children who are not saved. "It may take months or years of asking questions and putting the pieces together before God definitively calls a child to a point of decision."[13] Children like to please parents and other adults. Christian parents and adults want to

---

[11] William Craig Price, *Engage: Tools for Contemporary Evangelism* (New Orleans Baptist Theological Seminary, 2019), 309.

[12] Bill Emeott, ed., *What About Kids Ministry: Practical Answers to Questions about Kids Ministry* (B&H, 2018), 120.

[13] Emeott, 121.

be available to curious children, but they do not want to push a child to make a decision before he or she is ready.

Helping a Child with Discernment

How old were you when you became a Christian? Did you contemplate this decision? Did you ask questions about Christianity, Jesus, or God? As children are contemplating Christianity, leaders want to encourage their thoughts and questions. In the training manual, *Sharing God's Special Plan with Children,* three types of decisions are explained.[14]

The first decision is "a step toward God."[15] This is when an inquisitive child shows interest in becoming a Christian and is taking steps toward God but "does not have a clear concept of sin or accountability before God."[16] The adult should affirm the child's thoughts and questions. The adult should pray with the child, thanking God for the child and his or her interest in becoming a Christian.

The second decision is a "profession of faith."[17] The child has an understanding of Christianity and is ready to become a Christian. With this decision, an adult should present the gospel simply and sincerely. (The gospel presentation will be discussed in the next section.)

The third decision is the "assurance of salvation."[18] This decision is made when a child who is a Christian has strayed away from

---

[14] North American Mission Board, *Sharing God's Special Plan*, 12.
[15] North American Mission Board, 18.
[16] North American Mission Board, 12.
[17] North American Mission Board, 19.
[18] North American Mission Board, 20.

the Lord. The child may feel guilty and want to recommit his or her life to Christ. Some may call this decision a rededication of commitment.

Points to Consider When Presenting the Gospel to Children

First, prepare a personalized script. One of the greatest privileges for Christians is to see a non-believer accept Christ as Savior. However, for many Christians, presenting the gospel is overwhelming and nerve-racking, especially when speaking to children. The presenter worries that he or she will accidentally give wrong information or will lead people to decisions they are not ready to make.

Preparing a script is an excellent way to avoid the hazards of nervously presenting the gospel. Before creating one, consider personalizing a script written by Christian childhood educators. These can be found from various organizations. For example, Lifeway Kids of Lifeway Christian Resources provides scripts, tracts, and tools that can be used when presenting the gospel to children. In my seminary classes, students are assigned to write, practice, and present their personalized gospel presentations in class. The students are given a script from the Lifeway website as an example. They may choose to personalize the example or write one from scratch. Then students are instructed to practice reading their scripts at home in front of a mirror. Next, they practice with a child who is already a Christian. The child lets the student know if he or she understands the presentation. Finally, the students bring their prepared scripts to class where they practice with other students. Continually practicing presenting the gospel so that the words become a natural part of conversations for the presenter is important. When the presenter is at ease, the receiving person will feel at ease. Hopefully, this gives the receiving person the freedom to accept the gospel when ready.

Second, use tracts and visual aids. The use of tracts and visual aids when presenting the gospel to children can be helpful. Children enjoy visual aids. Choose one that is designed for children and is not wordy. A wordy tract or tool is cumbersome to use. One Bible verse per point is best. When two or more verses are read, the presenter or the child can become distracted or overwhelmed.

The tracts that Lifeway produces for Vacation Bible School are excellent tools. These have updated graphics with child-friendly language. If a tract is not available, the Romans Road presentation is good to use with children. The verses are Rom 3:10; 5:8; 6:23; 10:9–10; and 10:13.

Third, encourage parents to be a part of the conversation. Churches who invest in children provide many opportunities for them to learn about Christ. Typically, churches offer programs such as Bible study, children's or family worship, Vacation Bible School, and camp, among other events. These programs are led by staff and volunteers who devote their time to teach children about the Christian life. Each person should be trained to share the gospel with a child.

Parents should be trained and ready to help a child become a Christian. While the church supports the family, the parents are the most influential people in a child's life.[19] Therefore, parents should

---

[19] Christian Smith and Amy Adamczyk, *Handing Down the Faith: How Parents Pass Their Religion on to the Next Generation* (Oxford University Press, 2021), 69.

know how to assist their children in making a decision to become a Christian. The training of parents and volunteers is an important responsibility for a church staff.

Putting It All Together

The discussion of salvation begins with the child. When a child asks questions or discusses becoming a Christian, consider the following:

1. Determine the intent of the conversation. Is the child wanting to become a Christian?
    a. If yes, continue the conversation.
    b. If no, answer the child's questions to his or her content.
2. Determine the understanding of the child. Does the child know the answers to the following?
    a. What is sin? (Sin is "actions, attitudes, words, or thoughts that do not please God.")[20]
    b. Who sins? (Everyone sins.)
    c. When we sin, whom do we sin against? (We sin against God.)
    d. What happens when we sin against God? (We are separated from him.)
    e. What did Jesus do for us and why? (Jesus died on the cross to take the punishment for our sins. He arose from the grave and is our living Savior. He did this because he loves us.)
3. If the child can answer each of these questions in his or her own words, ask the child if he or she is ready to become a

[20] Holmes and Latham, *Holman Illustrated Bible Dictionary for Kids*, 179.

Christian. If the answer is yes, present the gospel simply and sincerely. If the answer is no, tell the child that when he or she is ready to become a Christian, you will be ready to have another conversation. Pray for the child before ending the conversation. Always affirm a child's interest in Christ.

4. When presenting the gospel, remember to do the following:
   a. Use words the child will understand.
   b. Encourage the child to answer and ask questions. Engage the child in the conversation.
   c. Ask open-ended questions.
   d. Listen intently to the child's words.
   e. Do not pressure the child into a decision.
5. At the conclusion of the gospel presentation, invite the child to ask Jesus into his or her life.
   a. If the answer is yes, help the child respond in prayer. It is important for children to use their own words; however, some children may want guidance. Guide the child to admit to God that he or she has sinned and is sorry for his or her sins. Remind the child to tell God that he or she believes Jesus is God's Son. Guide the child to tell God that Jesus is his or her Savior and Lord. When children say their own prayers rather than repeating someone else's words, they are more likely to take the commitment seriously.[21] Include the parents as much as possible, inviting them to be in the room with the child as the prayer is being said.

---

[21] Beth Bowman et al., *I'm a Christian Now!* (Lifeway Christian Resources, 2015), 61.

   b. If the answer is no, affirm the child in taking a step toward God. Pray for the child and communicate that you are always available to talk about becoming a Christian. Mention that God will help the child know when he or she is ready to become a Christian.

6. After the child prays, remind him or her of Heb 13:5—Jesus will never leave or abandon us. Help the child understand that once a person becomes a Christian, he or she will never have to make this decision again. It is a lifelong decision.
7. Help the child think of a way to commemorate this special day. Write the date in the child's Bible, write in a journal about the experience of becoming a Christian, take a family photo, or think of other ways. [22]
8. Discuss the next step with the child: baptism. Explain that baptism is a way to tell others about one's decision to become a Christian.

Follow-up

The decision to follow Jesus is the most significant one a person will ever make. Because of the magnitude of this decision, follow-up is vital. Follow-up should involve the following:

1. The church leader should contact the parent immediately following a child's decision to become a Christian. While parents should be involved in this process, sometimes the decision is made at camp or at other church events when the parent is not present.

[22] Bowman et al., 61.

2. The children's minister and/or pastor should visit the home within two weeks of the child's decision. They should speak with the child and parents concerning baptism, allowing time for questions and affirming the decision to become a follower of Christ.
3. The church leaders should teach a new Christians class. During this class, children will learn the importance of church membership, baptism, the Lord's Supper, and continual growth in Christ.
4. A discipleship plan to help children grow in their faith by learning the spiritual disciplines and the importance of the Christian community is essential.

Conclusion

Children are amazing creatures made in the image of God. The psalmist writes, "I will praise you because I have been remarkably and wondrously made" (Ps 139:14). Jesus said, "Truly I tell you, . . . unless you turn and become like little children, you will never enter the kingdom of heaven" (Matt 18:3). Childlike faith is necessary to become a Christian. One must simply believe. "Children, especially in their personal relationship with Jesus, are even more receptive, yes, more understanding than adults. For many adults are used to listening superficially, while little ones do not miss the smallest or most insignificant thing."[23] Helping a child become a Christian is one of the greatest occurrences in the life of a believer.

---

[23] Christoph Blumhardt and Johann Blumhardt, *Thoughts about Children* (Plough, 1980), 20.

Discussion Questions

1. What should a child understand before becoming a Christian? Discuss each of the five points. Are there other points to consider?
2. Communicating with a child is not the same as communicating with an adult. What should an adult consider when sharing the gospel with children?
3. Name the three types of decisions a child can make. Differentiate each one.
4. Describe a salvation conversation with a child.
5. Why is follow-up with a child important?

Opportunities for Application

- Provide training for parents and all adults who work with elementary children on how to have gospel conversations with children. Never assume that adults or parents know how to share the gospel with children. Gospel conversations require training.
- Regularly offer a new Christians class for children. Typically, these classes are six to eight weeks. Lifeway Kids publishes a new Christian curriculum for children.
- When children make the decision to follow Christ, it is good to help them make this decision memorable. As children grow into teens, they doubt many parts of their lives, including their faith. As a pastor, children's minister, or parent, how can you make the decision to become a Christian memorable for a child?

CHAPTER 5

Salvation for Children with Disabilities

Sandra Peoples

In the late 1990s, my big sister walked the aisle at First Baptist Church in Duncan, Oklahoma, and told Brother Brad that she had accepted Jesus as her Savior and wanted to be baptized. Even though she was the oldest sibling in our family, she was the last one to make this decision, and we all rejoiced with her. She could not answer every question Brother Brad usually asked teenagers when they committed their lives to following Jesus, but she understood that Jesus loved her and that he forgave her of her sins.

When she passed away a couple of years ago, she left behind dozens of journals with notes she took during sermons as well as prayers she wrote down for herself and others. Her faith looked a lot like it did on that Sunday morning almost thirty years before. She would probably answer the same questions in the same way she did then—Jesus loved her and forgave her, and that was enough.

My sister had Down syndrome, an intellectual, developmental disability that affected her motor skills and her cognitive abilities, but it did not stop her from putting her faith in Jesus and following him. Her testimony and her example mean more to me than that of any expert theologian or educated pastor (amen!). Matt 5:8 says, "Blessed are the pure in heart, for they will see God," and she could certainly be described as pure in heart. I trust that she is now with the saints before the throne of God, worshipping him for eternity.

Having grown up with a sister with Down syndrome is the catalyst for my current ministry calling—helping churches take steps of accessibility so people with disabilities and their families can attend. We grew up in a church that modeled that well, which is why my sisters and I were all able to attend each week, hear the gospel, and be baptized. If they had not accepted her and made accommodations, it would have changed our family for future generations.

My advocacy continues because I have a son with level-three autism and intellectual disabilities. He is functionally nonverbal, so even though he is the same age as my sister when she was saved and baptized, he is not able to articulate his faith and understanding even at the level of her ability. But that does not stop our church from speaking the gospel over him, teaching him the Bible, giving him opportunities to be in community with friends, and praying for his salvation and sanctification.

This chapter addresses salvation for children with disabilities. As you have read, this is not just theoretical for me. It is about my sister and my son and how Jesus works in their lives to draw them into a relationship with himself. The discussion starts by looking at what it means to be made in the image of God as well as addressing sin and the effects it has on those who are sinful but may not be seen as guilty. This chapter will also explore the role of ministry leaders in the lives of children with disabilities. Ministry leaders can help children have the opportunity to hear and respond to the best of their abilities. Ultimately, because children with disabilities (like all children) are made in the image of God, they have the potential to have a relationship with him and grow in Christlikeness. Our role as ministry leaders with children with disabilities is the same as it is with all children: present the gospel to them, pray for the Spirit to work in their lives, and trust God for their salvation.

The Image of God in Everyone

Genesis starts with the creation of everything in the world that is known to us, and the culmination of that creation is man:

> So God created man
> in his own image;
> he created him in the image of God;
> he created them male and female. (Gen 1:27)

Exactly what it means to be made in the image of God cannot be fully understood by fallen human beings.[1] But we can see consistent threads throughout Scripture that lead us to points of agreement. The relationship between the members of the Trinity is one thread. As they exist in fellowship and unity with each other, we too can be in fellowship with God and have unity with other believers.[2]

---

[1] Joel R. Beeke and Paul M. Smalley, *Reformed Systematic Theology, Volume 2: Man and Christ* (Crossway, 2020), chap. 10, Kindle.

[2] See Jesus's High Priestly Prayer in John 17.

John Kilner writes, "Being made in the image of God involves connection and reflection. Creation in God's image entails a special connection with God and also God's intention that people be a meaningful reflection of God, to God's glory."[3] John Hammett agrees: "The image of God is *the capacity of human beings to have a relationship with God*."[4] As we can see, the *imago Dei* is not dependent on functional abilities but is based on a model of reflecting Christ and connecting with God (through salvation and sanctification) and others (through friendship and church family).

People do not gain more of the image of God as they develop or meet certain criteria. It is true of us regardless of how we exhibit that image. We are fearfully and wonderfully made from conception by the loving and purposeful hands of our Creator.[5] James Estep writes, "As humans, we develop throughout our lifespan and in various areas of measurable progress such as cognitive, social, moral, or personality—as reflected by numerous theories. Yet innate to our humanity is that we are God's image-bearers. We do not *develop* into the *imago Dei*; we *are* the *imago Dei*."[6] And Jeff McNair and Ben Rhodes expand on the idea: "The Bible applies to all people equally; all humans are originally created in the image of God, which is an ontological statement that does not exclude

---

[3] John F. Kilner, *Dignity and Destiny: Humanity in the Image of God* (Eerdmans, 2015), 311.

[4] John S. Hammett, "Human Nature" in *A Theology for the Church*, ed. by Daniel L. Akin (B&H Academic, 2014), 320.

[5] Psalm 139:13–14: "For it was you who created my inward parts; you knit me together in my mother's womb. I will praise you because I have been remarkably and wondrously made."

[6] James R. Estep Jr., "Christian Anthropology: Humanity as the *Imago Dei*" in *Christian Formation: Integrating Theology & Human Development*, ed. James R. Estep and Jonathan H. Kim (B&H Academic, 2010), 29.

any individual based on capacity (or incapacity). The dignity and determination, rights and responsibilities, privileges and pathos, of being human are not earned by the potential or actual exercise of particular abilities or characteristics."[7] This truth applies to infants in the womb, to children with disabilities, and through every age and stage people may reach.

One passage that is specific to people with disabilities is Moses's conversation with God about his calling and limitations. Exodus 4 may be a surprising place to look for an answer to the question about salvation, but it is a clear passage about God's role in creating people with disabilities. This scene is at the burning bush, where God called Moses to speak before Pharaoh and lead his people out of Egypt. Moses did not believe he was up to the calling and used his own design as a reason he could not fulfill the role:

> But Moses replied to the Lord, "Please, Lord, I have never been eloquent—either in the past or recently or since you have been speaking to your servant—because my mouth and my tongue are sluggish."
>
> The Lord said to him, "Who placed a mouth on humans? Who makes a person mute or deaf, seeing or blind? Is it not I, the Lord? Now go! I will help you speak and I will teach you what to say." (Exod 4:10–12)

God took credit for disabilities, saying they fulfill his purpose. Michael Beates writes, "We have discovered that God is not only creator of man and we are made *imago Dei*, but we have seen that

---

[7] Jeff McNair and Ben Rhodes, "Towards a Christian Model of Disability: The Bible Is for All People," *Journal of the Christian Institute on Disability* 8, no. 1 (Spring/Summer 2019): 21.

God is declared to be the creator of disabilities."[8] This same idea is reflected in John 9, when the disciples asked why the man they passed was born blind and Jesus responded, "So that God's works might be displayed in him" (v. 3). In this passage, the man born blind had more insight into who Jesus was than the Pharisees who could see. As Ben Rhodes writes, "It is the man born blind who truly sees Jesus—recognizes and confesses him as Lord—whereas the physically sighted Pharisees are unable to see Jesus."[9]

We all reflect the image of God through our ability to have a relationship with him and as we grow more like Christ, who is the perfect image of God. This potential is true for children with disabilities as well. And what holds them back from this potential holds us all back as well, but it may look different in their lives than in the lives of those who are typically developing.

Sin and Guilt

We know that "all have sinned and fall short of the glory of God" (Rom 3:23), but are all people guilty of sin in the same way? Does God take age, stage of development, and cognitive ability into consideration? The topic of people with disabilities and salvation can be discussed along with the eternal destiny of infants and children who die before they are able to make a profession of faith. Are they guilty when they are unable to understand the sinfulness of their actions? Let us look at three passages that help us see young children as God sees them.

---

[8] Michael S. Beates, *Disability and The Gospel: How God Uses Our Brokenness to Display His Grace* (Crossway, 2012), 77.

[9] Ben Rhodes, "Signs and Wonders: Disability in the Fourth Gospel," *Journal of the Christian Institute on Disability* 5, no. 1 (Spring/Summer, 2016): 65.

First, the Israelite infants and children were not guilty of the sins of the older generations as they traveled to the Promised Land. Deut 1:39 says, "Your children, who you said would be plunder, your sons who don't yet know good from evil, will enter there. I will give them the land, and they will take possession of it." The children did not suffer the consequences of the sin in which they did not participate. Second, we read that Samuel was not expected to know the voice of God because he was young and the Lord had not been revealed to him: "Now Samuel did not yet know the Lord, because the word of the Lord had not yet been revealed to him" (1 Sam 3:7). The third example is from the life of David. He was told that the baby Bathsheba was carrying would die (2 Sam 12:14), and he pleaded with the Lord to spare his child's life. But when he was told the baby had died, he said, "I'll go to him, but he will never return to me" (12:23b). David seemed to understand that his child would be with God after his death.

Sin entered the world through Adam, and "death through sin[;] in this way death spread to all people, because all sinned" (Rom 5:12). But the examples above show that not everyone is guilty of sin in the same way. Infants and young children are sinful but not guilty, and this applies to those with disabilities as well. As Adam Harwood writes, "People fall under God's judgment when they are capable of moral action, which implies that there is an earlier period of time in which people are not capable of moral action."[10] Albert Mohler and Daniel Akin point us to 2 Cor 5:10 on the topic of the guilt of "little ones," which we can apply to infants and people with profound disabilities. This passage says, "For we must all appear before the

---

[10] Adam Harwood, *The Spiritual Condition of Infants: A Biblical-Historical Survey and Systematic Proposal* (Wipf & Stock, 2011), 154.

judgment seat of Christ, so that each may be repaid for what he has done in the body, whether good or evil." Mohler and Akin write, "We will face the judgment seat of Christ and be judged, not on the basis of original sin, but for our sins committed during our own lifetimes. Each will answer 'according to what he has done,' and not for the sin of Adam."[11]

Most children grow to understand their sin and are held accountable, just as Samuel was as he grew (1 Sam 3:19). They are called to confess and believe to be saved (Rom 10:9). But some people, like those with intellectual developmental disabilities, are unable to understand at the same rate or level as typical children and may be unable to verbalize what they understand. In this, God "is patient with you, not wanting any to perish but all to come to repentance" (2 Pet 3:9).

Trusting Their Creator with Their Salvation

In Acts 16:30, the Philippian jailer asked Paul and Silas, "What must I do to be saved?" What must a child with disabilities do to be saved? Although God's answer to this question does not change, the application of the truth takes each person's development into consideration. As John Swinton writes, "The assumption that our relationship with God is in any way dependent on the presence or absence of human capabilities is a theological mistake."[12]

---

[11] R. Albert Mohler Jr. and Daniel L. Akin, "The Salvation of the 'Little Ones': Do Infants who Die Go to Heaven?" AlbertMohler.com, The Southern Baptist Theological Seminary, https://albertmohler.com/2009/07/16/the-salvation-of-the-little-ones-do-infants-who-die-go-to-heaven/.

[12] John Swinton, "Known by God," in *The Paradox of Disability: Responses to Jean Vanier and L'Arche Communities from Theology and the Sciences*, ed. Hans S. Reinders (Eerdmans, 2010), 144.

There are many children with developmental disabilities who can come to faith through the conviction of their sins, an understanding of their need, and an expression of their faith, no matter how simple that expression. Billy Graham wrote, "I could not help thinking how kind and understanding and compassionate God has been in choosing to reveal Himself to man through simple childlike faith rather than the intellect. There would otherwise be no chance for little children or the [cognitively impaired]."[13] God calls, convicts, and converts, and those who are able to understand their sin and respond can receive the gift of faith through the work of the Holy Spirit: "For you are saved by grace through faith, and this is not from yourselves; it is God's gift—not from works, so that no one can boast" (Eph 2:8–9).

But what about children who may never be able to articulate their understanding and faith? Does this exclude them from the opportunity for salvation and a relationship with God? John Hammett would say it does not exclude them. In fact, he writes, "Seeing our capacity for relationship with God as dependent on spirit leaves open the possibilities that God can establish relationships with humans in exceptional ways in exceptional circumstances, such as when reason is impaired, or no longer functioning, or not yet functioning."[14] The authors of *The Reciprocating Self* add to this view:

> We believe that the religious and spiritual development trajectory is unique for all people based on their individual (e.g., biological, psychological) factors and their relations

[13] Billy Graham, *How to Be Born Again* (Word, 1989), 148.

[14] John S. Hammett, "A Whole Bible Approach to Interpreting Creation in God's Image," *Southwestern Journal of Theology: The Doctrine of Humankind* 63, no. 2 (Spring 2021): 38.

> with their contexts (e.g., cultural, religious). Despite these diverse expressions, we argue that the developmental trajectory of reciprocating spirituality is toward coherence of experiences of transcendence, fidelity and one's way of living in the world.[15]

Many with profound intellectual disabilities are not able to read Scripture, understand the gospel as it is preached in churches, or verbally respond to an invitation, yet they can be drawn by the Holy Spirit.

God is love and desires to have a relationship with everyone he created. It is against his character to create people with disabilities who would be unable to have a relationship with him. As Reinders states, "Because of who God is and what God does, we know that profoundly disabled human beings are children of God and are as loveable in his eyes as any other of his children."[16] McNair and Rhodes point out that how people with disabilities obtain salvation is not that different from everyone else:

> All people, regardless of capacity, need this salvation (Romans 3:23) which precisely cannot be achieved through anything any of us are able to accomplish. Grace is not dependent on our individual capacity, talent, or ability, all of which vary from person to person (even within the lifespan and circumstances of an individual life). The invitation to the family of God is made to all, and the name of God's children, brothers

---

[15] Jack O. Balswick et al., *The Reciprocating Self: Human Development in Theological Perspective*, 2nd ed. (IVP, 2016), 328.

[16] Hans S. Reinders, *Receiving the Gift of Friendship: Profound Disability, Theological Anthropology, and Ethics* (Eerdmans, 2008), 275.

and sisters in Christ, is extended to all who respond in faith (1 John 3:1–2; Galatians 3:26).[17]

The same Holy Spirit who drew each one of us to himself and into a salvific relationship is also at work in people with intellectual disabilities. And they can follow the same pattern for salvation we do. Paul made this clear in Phil 1:6: "I am sure of this, that he who started a good work in you will carry it on to completion until the day of Christ Jesus." God begins the good work, and he brings it to completion. God knows what is required to have salvation in Christ through faith, and he has known the path and potential for every person he created (Ps 139:13–16). He alone knows what he would require from each one. We do not have to have all the answers to be faithful to our calling in the lives of children with disabilities.

Our Role as Ministry Leaders

Applying what we have learned about the image of God, the guilt of sin, and the potential for salvation is important to me both as a ministry leader and a mom. At church, I teach our specialized, sensory-friendly class. The children in my class have developmental disabilities, cognitive impairments, and limited verbal ability. At home, my son is able to repeat "Amen" at the end of a prayer but cannot tell me what he believes about the God who hears us. But my calling as a teacher and as a mom is not any different than it was when I was teaching a class of typical first and second graders or when I was praying with my older son who is now in college. That calling is the Great Commandment and the Great Commission—to

[17] McNair and Rhodes, "Towards a Christian Model of Disability," 22.

love God and love others and to teach my students and my sons to do the same. As ministry leaders and volunteers, we can be aware of the limitations children with disabilities have while also making our church environments for them about more than just babysitting them while their families are being discipled. We can disciple them as well!

For the youngest ages and the most profoundly disabled, we can show Christ's love as we care for their needs and speak simple truths of the gospel over them. In the class I teach, I pick a simple three-to-four-word phrase to focus on during our time together, like "God made everything." Then I apply it to the activities we do and the conversations we have—for example, saying, "God made Joshua's arms so strong!" as a child throws a ball or saying, "God made ducks that say 'quack, quack'" as we do a puzzle. As the children grow, we adapt our curriculum to meet their needs using PECS (Picture Exchange Communication System) images and simple versions of Bible stories. Consistency is comforting to children with disabilities, so we keep the same schedule and often listen to the same songs each week or watch the same video clips. When our students smile when they hear a song or when they are able to repeat a phrase or the main idea of the lesson, we know the Holy Spirit is at work in their hearts!

Children who are developmentally delayed but have the verbal ability to communicate and participate can spend time in both our specialized class and the typical class with their peers, where we take steps of inclusion so they can participate to the best of their abilities. That can include modifying the sensory environment, behavior expectations, and opportunities for engagement in the lesson. All of these steps have the same goal—teaching the gospel.

When Jesus said, "Let the little children come to me. Don't stop them, because the kingdom of God belongs to such as these" in Mark 10:14, he did not refer only to the children who can quietly sit crisscross on a carpet square through a Bible lesson, read from their storybook Bibles, memorize John 3:16, or answer all the questions on the activity sheet. In fact, in Paul's description of the church, greater honor is given to those who seem to be weaker. He writes, ". . . those parts of the body that are weaker are indispensable" (1 Cor 12:22). Let us, as ministry leaders, recognize the potential in our children who may seem weaker and support them as Jesus would have done.

In Matthew 25, Jesus spoke of separating the sheep from the goats, the true followers of him from the others. He said a mark of his true followers was to offer food and drink to those in need, to clothe the naked, to care for the sick, and to visit those in prison. Scripture says,

> Then the righteous will answer him, "Lord, when did we see you hungry and feed you, or thirsty and give you something to drink? When did we see you a stranger and take you in, or without clothes and clothe you? When did we see you sick, or in prison, and visit you?'
>
> And the King will answer them, "Truly I tell you, whatever you did for one of the least of these brothers and sisters of mine, you did for me." (vv. 37–40)

We honor Jesus when we serve those in need, and children with disabilities and their families are certainly in need of the gospel and a church family who cares for them. As Syble's sister and James's mom, I want to say thank you for reading this chapter and learning more about our stories. I hope you better understand the potential children with disabilities have to experience salvation so that you can take steps to include them and their families. What a joy it will be in heaven when they are free from everything that holds them back in this life and can worship God in perfect fellowship with other believers!

Discussion Questions

1. How do you understand the image of God? Do your ideas apply to everyone regardless of cognitive ability?
2. As you read the three Scripture passages on children who are sinful but not held accountable for sins they did not commit, do you agree with the author's application? Why or why not? Are there other biblical examples you can list to support your view?
3. How could what the world might consider weaknesses in the life of a person with a disability actually be strengths when it comes to one's faith?
4. What action steps has this chapter brought to mind as you minister to children with disabilities? What curriculum or resources do you need to take those steps? What is your plan for finding those resources?

Opportunities for Application

- Consider specialized plans for children with disabilities in your church.
- To disciple children with disabilities, many churches borrow a concept from special education in schools and apply it to the church context. The author's church created individual discipleship plans (IDP). Similar to what schools use for students with disabilities (an individual education plan [IEP]), an IDP takes a child's strengths, challenges, and potential into consideration to set goals for growing in Christlikeness.

- Consider setting IDP goals in five different areas (prayer, Scripture memory, worship participation, Bible lesson participation and application, and social/behavior expectations). Talk about the goals as a ministry team and set up a meeting with parents (and the child if he/she is able) so everyone is in agreement with the plan. Evaluate the goals and update them at the end of each school year, especially when the child is moving to a new room or new environment (like from preschool to elementary school or from children's ministry to the youth group).
- To use the example of setting a goal in the area of prayer, some options to consider include the following: saying "Amen" when the teacher is done praying aloud, repeating a simple prayer at snack time, sharing one prayer request when it is one's turn, or leading the class in prayer. As the child grows and develops more skills, adjust the expectations to grow as well. IDPs are a helpful tool for remembering that children with disabilities can be discipled, even if that requires a different plan from what is in place for a majority of children in the classroom.

CHAPTER 6

Baptism and Children

Malcolm B. Yarnell III

When we think of the baptism of children, we should consider the same basic truths as when we think of the baptism of adults. After all, Jesus and the apostles made no exceptions or qualifications regarding the baptism of children. However, Jesus spoke both about children and about baptism, so we must synthesize his teachings on both matters. After a careful review of the biblical evidence, we may begin to address how best to baptize children today.

First, let us consider what the Lord Jesus Christ has to say about children. Second, let us consider what the Lord has to say about baptism. Third, only after we have heard the Word of God about both children and baptism should we attempt to craft a doctrine of the baptism of children. Finally, we can then look at the practice of the baptism of children.

The Lord's Teaching About Children

The first thing to notice about the Lord's view of children is how much he sought to bless them with his presence. The attitude of Jesus toward children stands in stark contrast to the attitudes of the earliest disciples toward children. Indeed, Jesus had to teach the disciples that they must bless the children and learn to be like children. The apostle Mark writes about one significant episode in which Jesus Christ showed how the church must view and treat children.

> People were bringing little children to him in order that he might touch them, but the disciples rebuked them. When Jesus saw it, he was indignant and said to them, "Let the little children come to me. Don't stop them, because the kingdom of God belongs to such as these. Truly I tell you, whoever does not receive the kingdom of God like a little child will never enter it." After taking them in his arms, he laid his hands on them and blessed them. (Mark 10:13–16)

The Gospel of Mark tells us that "people" (probably parents, grandparents, and/or guardians) were trying to bring their *paidia* to Jesus. *Paidion* was the Greek term for a small child, even an infant. The disciples seem to have organized who could approach the Lord, since at this point everyone wanted to speak to him (cf. John 12:20–22). Since he was busy teaching great truths, healing those who were sick, and even raising people from death, the disciples probably rejected the children. Perhaps they deemed children an imposition on their Master's time. "These children don't need the Lord since they don't seem to be sick, and infants cannot really understand what he's teaching anyway."

However, Jesus became "indignant" when he saw the children being turned away. The Lord corrected his disciples and turned the incident into a teaching episode for the benefit of all his followers, including us today. In this episode, Jesus demonstrated three great truths about children: (1) He wants children to come to him; (2) children by faith know how to enter the kingdom, and (3) he wants to bless the children.

Jesus Wants Every Child to Come to Him

First, Jesus commanded the disciples, "Let the little children come to me. Don't stop them." To come between the Lord and the people whom he wants to bless is a terrible thing. Jesus did not come just to bless adults. He also came to bless children, even the littlest ones! Children were a priority to Jesus, and they must be a priority to all his followers. The church must make children a priority, and that priority begins with introducing the children to Jesus. This is why we must be diligent to tell the children about God—about who he is and about what he has done, continues to do, and will do.

Childlike Faith is Necessary for Salvation

Second, the Lord taught his disciples some important things about the nature of saving faith by using the children in an object lesson. Jesus subtly but surely removed any sense of superiority the disciples may have had in their attitude toward the children. He said that the children instinctively know how to enter the kingdom of God, and the one who wants to enter heaven must do so "like" a small child. Jesus had already taught them that salvation comes by faith. Then, he extolled a child as an exemplar of faith. Perhaps they were reminded that every person is entirely dependent on divine grace for gaining (and maintaining) his or her place in the kingdom. The only proper response a person can have to the Lord's gift of salvation is the receiving attitude of faith.

Salvation is not something a person can do for himself or herself. Everyone who would enter the kingdom of God must do so like an infant. Remember how our babies are entirely dependent on us for their very lives? At every moment they remain small, vulnerable, and subject to another. Little children are the recipients of everything they need to live, from food to shelter to cleanliness. The second verse of "Rock of Ages," a hymn written by the famous eighteenth-century Puritan Augustus Toplady, captures the proper attitude that every person must possess to receive life from God:

> Not the labors of my hands
> Can fulfill Thy law's demands;
> These for sin could not atone;
> Thou must save, and Thou alone:
> In my hand no price I bring,
> Simply to Thy cross I cling.[1]

Jesus Wants to Bless the Children

The third great truth that Jesus taught his disciples during this encounter concerned his desire to "bless" the children. Jesus "touched" the little children in the same way that the priests and kings of Israel and the leaders of the NT churches were set apart and received grace to perform their important ministries—by laying on of hands. In a day when we have become all too aware that not everyone who

---

[1] Augustus M. Toplady, "Rock of Ages," in *The Baptist Hymnal*, ed. Wesley L. Forbis (Convention Press, 1991), 342.

touches children intends to bless them, we have the contrary example of Jesus. Jesus did not touch in a harmful way but in a beneficial way. The physical "touch" of Jesus always brought a blessing, including the healing of those who were suffering (cf. Mark 3:10; 5:28; 6:56; 8:22). Today, the disciples of Jesus Christ must seek to bless children through bringing them to him for his touch. But where is Jesus today? Christ is "among" his covenanted congregation, for it has "gathered together" in his name (Matt 18:20).

Jesus said many other things about the children, but this one pericope from his earthly ministry teaches the basic attitude the people of God must have toward children. First, we must be careful to introduce the children to the Lord, recognizing that neglecting our ministry to the children is unacceptable to the Lord and worthy of rebuke. Second, we must be humble and look to children as an example of the way everyone must enter and remain in the kingdom of God, by grace through faith. And, finally, we must seek to bless the children by bringing them into the very presence of God in Christ for their spiritual healing and sustenance above all other things.

The Lord's Teaching About Baptism

As we shall demonstrate, the Lord and his apostles taught the following five major truths about baptism. First, water baptism and Spirit baptism are distinct, yet they should be correlative. Second, Christ filled the act of water baptism with his righteousness. Third, water baptism portrays a person's reception of the gospel of Jesus Christ. Fourth, Jesus commanded the baptism of believers. And fifth, baptism testifies to personal faith.

Water Baptism and Spirit Baptism

Before the ministry of Jesus began, John the Baptist told his followers that while he baptized with water, the Messiah's baptism would be different, for Christ would baptize them with the Holy Spirit (Mark 1:8). This indicates an irreducible difference between physical immersion in water and the reception of the Spirit. Physical baptism in water, which represents the new birth in Christ, must be distinguished from the actual gift of being born again by the Holy Spirit. However, water baptism and Spirit baptism, which accompanies faith in Christ and new life, still occur near each other in the NT (Acts 2:38; 10:47; 19:3–5; 22:16). Water baptism, a physical action, and Spirit baptism, which comes with salvation, are different but must correlate with one another.

Being "born again" by the Holy Spirit (John 3:1–5), which is also called being "baptized with the Holy Spirit" (Acts 11:16), occurs invisibly within a human being and is a work of God rather than a work of man. However, the external effect of this internal baptism by the Holy Spirit will be seen in a person's life (John 3:5–8). People receive water baptism with their bodies as an external witness to their personal repentance from sin and their internal reception "of the Holy Spirit" (Acts 2:38). Water baptism, which involves the external "removal of dirt from the body" does not save a person. Rather, "the pledge of a good conscience toward God" through faith in "the resurrection of Jesus Christ" is that which "now saves you" (1 Pet 3:21).

We can summarize the difference between water baptism and Spirit baptism in the NT teaching of Christ and his apostles with two equally true statements. These two truths may not be divided from one another nor conflated with one another. The following truths about baptism are deeply distinct but intimately intertwined: First, the baptism of the Spirit internally (and immediately) saves the person who repents toward God and believes in Jesus Christ. Second, the baptism of water, which is given by the church to the new Christian, witnesses externally to that person's internal salvation. Another way to say it is that internal baptism is the work of the Holy Spirit, while external baptism is the work of the church.

Christ Filled Baptism with His Righteousness

Jesus received water baptism from John the Baptist, but his reception of water baptism was different from that of any other human being. Jesus had no sin from which he needed to repent. And he is the one who gives the Spirit that every other human being must receive if he or she going to be united with him in salvation. Rather, Jesus underwent baptism so that he could "fulfill all righteousness" (Matt 3:15).

Verifying that his baptism was indeed the perfect and righteous baptism, each person of the Holy Trinity manifested himself at the baptism of Jesus. The Spirit descended in the form of a "dove," and the Father spoke aloud that he was pleased with his "beloved Son," who had just filled the act of baptism with his righteousness (vv. 16–17).

When a human being puts his or her faith in Jesus Christ as Lord, believing that he died and rose again for his or her salvation, that person receives Christ's righteousness (Rom 10:9–10). We are not justified by our own works, including the physical activity of water baptism, but by trusting Jesus Christ is Lord. "The righteous will live by faith" (Rom 1:16–17; cf. Hab 2:4). We become personally right with God through personal faith in Jesus Christ, in his death and in his resurrection.

So far, we have discovered two important aspects of the Lord's teaching on baptism. First, the external baptism of water is distinguished from yet must accompany the baptism of the Holy Spirit. Second, the activity of baptism was an act of repentance from sin for the followers of John the Baptist, but Jesus gave his righteousness to the Christian activity of baptism. True water baptism requires the baptism of the Holy Spirit, which accompanies personal faith in Christ and repentance toward God. However, we cannot stop with these two important aspects of baptism. Three other aspects of NT baptism require delineation.

Water Baptism Portrays the Gospel

The third major aspect we must incorporate in our teaching is that water baptism reflects the fundamental gospel facts of death and resurrection. This truth contains both death and life, both difficulty and victory, both ignominy and glory. There exists a dialectic between harshness and joyfulness, with the harshness preceding the joy. There is also a sense of a progress, of a journey which progresses through death into life. The triumph of Christ's resurrection followed the tragedy of his cross. It must be the same for his disciples. Our victory as his followers comes through the pain of discipleship. He paved the way through death into life, and we must follow him on that way, for he is "the Way." Indeed, the way of his humanity is the only way our humanity can enter his divine presence (John 14:6; cf. Heb 2:9–18).

On the hard side of this dialectic truth, we must face up to the reality of suffering and death. Jesus Christ made it clear that his baptism necessitated death. He warned his disciples that while they coveted the good things of his kingdom, suffering and death come before resurrection and glory (Mark 10:32–40). Jesus promised them that because they were his disciples, "You will be baptized with the baptism I am baptized with" (v. 39). The apostle Paul taught that the Christ follower must accept death as predestined by God. He asked the Roman Christians, "Or are you unaware that all of us who were baptized into Christ Jesus were baptized into his death?" (Rom 6:3; cf. Phil 1:29).

On the joyous side of this dialectic truth, we find our ultimate hope in the reality of resurrection and eternal life. The apostle Paul also taught that the disciple's death does not stand alone but is a mere precursor to life. The process of dying and arising from death with Christ is pictured perfectly in the baptism of a disciple of Jesus Christ. The Roman Christians were informed that death is temporary and that life rushes toward us through our death in Christ. Baptism portrays in a visual act the truth that the gospel proclaims in oral words: "Therefore we were buried with him by baptism into death, in order that, just as Christ was raised from the dead by the glory of the Father, so we too may walk in newness of life. For if we have been united with him in the likeness of his death, we will certainly also be in the likeness of his resurrection" (Rom 6:4–5).

Jesus Commanded the Baptism of Believers

After his death and resurrection, the risen Lord Jesus Christ commanded his disciples to baptize new believers. The Great Commission that he gave to his church requires our primary activity be to "make disciples." However, the subsidiary activities of "going," "teaching," and "baptizing" are also necessary. The Great Commission of the only Lord of the church states,

> Jesus came near and said to them, "All authority has been given to me in heaven and on earth. Go, therefore, and make disciples of all nations, baptizing them in the name of the Father and of the Son and of the Holy Spirit, teaching them to observe everything I have commanded you. And remember, I am with you always, to the end of the age." (Matt 28:18–20)

The activity of baptism comes as the church disperses to the nations to make disciples. The order, as the great Anabaptist theologian Balthasar Hubmaier noted, is both unalterable and significant: Go—make disciples—baptize. He also correctly associated the order of the Great Commission of Jesus in Matthew 28 with the order of the process of receiving salvation according to Paul in Romans 10. The true making of a disciple depends on the preaching of the Word of God and its reception by personal faith. "So faith comes through preaching, preaching, however, through the Word of God."[2]

Once a person has become a disciple, only then should he or she be baptized. The sequence commanded by the eternal Word of God may never be subjected to alteration by his followers, just as the written Word of God may not be altered (cf. Rev 22:18–19). After reviewing the biblical evidence for the sequence to be followed, Hubmaier said it well, "From these words one understands clearly and certainly that this sending of the apostles consists of three points or commands: first, preaching; second, faith; and third, outward baptism."[3]

[2] Balthasar Hubmaier, *On the Christian Baptism of Believers*, in *Balthasar Hubmaier: Theologian of Anabaptism*, trans. and ed. H. Wayne Pipkin and John H. Yoder (Herald, 1989), 116.

[3] Hubmaier, *On the Christian Baptism of Believers*, 115.

Water baptism testifies that personal faith is present in the recipient. Water baptism does not force the Holy Spirit upon the recipient. The baptism of the Holy Spirit occurs with true personal conversion, which itself is comprised of repentance and faith. Only the Spirit can bring this about (John 3:5–8). This internal work of salvation, which uses the human preaching of the Word in an entirely instrumental way (Rom 10:14–17), is a "monergistic" work of God and not a "synergistic" work that depends on the church or on some extrabiblical priesthood of the church.[4]

Baptism Testifies to Personal Faith

In other words, conversion is due entirely to divine grace and is not subject to direct or shared human causation. The Lord uses the church's preaching of the Word to bring conversion, but the church cannot force conversion through water baptism. Earlier in this chapter, we noted a person becomes personally right with God only through personal faith in Jesus Christ, as the Word calls the individual to exercise his or her own belief in Christ's death and resurrection by the influence of the Holy Spirit.

The activity of personal faith involves both the memory and the will of a human being. In other words, personal faith is composed of

---

[4] "Monergism" is a soteriological term that conveys the idea that salvation is the work of God alone. "Synergism" states that salvation is the work of both God and man. John Barclay contends for a third category, "energism," which approaches the "crucified monergism" I have advocated for elsewhere. Malcolm B. Yarnell III, "Crucified Monergism: A Theological Interpretation of Justification in Galatians," in *Justified in Jesus Christ: Evangelicals and Catholics in Dialogue*, ed. Steven Hoskins and David Fleischacker (University of Mary Press, 2017), 83–100; John Barclay, *Paul and the Gift* (Eerdmans, 2015), 442, 492, 518–19.

what might be called "personal knowledge" and "personal consent." Faith also has emotional consequences, which come to a human person either instantaneously or after some delay, but we shall focus here on the mind and the will rather than on the emotions of a person.

Personal knowledge concerns the truth about Jesus Christ, about who he is and about what he has done. He is the Son of God, and he became a human being to die on the cross and arise from the dead to save those who believe in him. But knowledge of the gospel alone is insufficient (Jas 2:19).

Personal consent describes an act of the will as reflected in the conscience. As an act of will, which is testified by the conscience, the gospel cannot be forced on a person by external human forces but must be received by faith through divine grace. The "conscience," moreover, witnesses to its genuine conversion through the believer's personal reception of water baptism (1 Pet 3:21).

According to the apostle Paul, the human conscience will be shown to have been made directly responsible to God "on the day," that is, on the day of judgment (Rom 2:16). The human mind, including the conscience, currently testifies to the eternal truth of God (1:18–21) and to the law God has made evident to our minds (2:12–15). Theologians refer to the presence of the knowledge of God in every human being through their conscience as "general revelation."[5]

Holy Scripture makes it thoroughly clear that we are each held accountable for our own personal actions. The prophet Ezekiel

[5] For a popular treatment of general revelation and natural law in the conscience, see Malcolm B. Yarnell III, *God*, Theology for Every Person, vol. 1 (B&H, 2024), 127–66. For an academic treatment, see David S. Dockery and Malcolm B. Yarnell III, *Special Revelation and Scripture*, Theology for the People of God (B&H Academic, 2024), 45–90.

describes multiple generations of both evil and righteousness so that he might show how every human being is responsible for his or her own sin. Everyone will be deemed either right with God or subject to damnation according to his or her own actions in mind and body. "The person who sins is the one who will die" (Ezek 18:4). The apostle John's description of the final judgment at "the great white throne" likewise demonstrates personal responsibility for personal actions (Rev 20:11–15).

In conclusion, Scripture intimately associates the practice of water baptism with the conscience of the human being receiving baptism. The internal conscience testifies before God to what we have thought about and consented to in this life. The external act of baptism testifies before human beings that we have consented to follow Jesus Christ. The witness of the conscience before God and the witness of water baptism before human beings must remain linked. Without that linkage, water baptism lacks integrity before God and man.

A Theology of Child Baptism

To summarize the truths learned from Scripture as we craft our doctrine of children and baptism is now both possible and beneficial. Two great truths immediately impress themselves from this review of the biblical witness. First, the Lord wants the little children to come to him, so his disciples must bring the children to him. Second, the Lord commanded the church to make disciples then baptize them. Every person is therefore called to come to Christ in personal faith and repentance. Water baptism is the external testimony to a person's true faith in Christ and baptism by the Spirit.

These two truths require constant attention as they are applied in the churches. The first requires us to share the gospel of Jesus Christ with the children in our spheres of influence. The second requires us to offer water baptism only to those who are born again. In other words, when the biblical theology of children and the biblical theology of baptism are brought together, we are required both to engage in intentional evangelistic conversations with children and to engage in sensitive listening to their responses.

However, it appears that Southern Baptists are not as careful as we should be. James Leo Garrett Jr. showed in 1991 how Southern Baptists were progressively baptizing children at younger ages. He raised the alarm that when believer's baptism is undermined, "the once-for-all character of true baptism is lost, and the demarcation between unbelief and faith, between church and world, between Christian lifestyle and pagan, between Christ and culture is blurred."[6] A denominational task force in 2014 expressed concern about that same continuing trend, finding "the only consistently growing age group in Southern Baptist Convention baptisms is 5 and under."[7]

Perhaps the impetus for child baptisms comes from the desire to shore up the general decline in numbers of baptisms in the churches. Or perhaps the cause is to be found in the lack of pastoral sensitivity when giving counsel to children who express an interest in being saved. Then again, perhaps the problem lies with parents who are eager to ensure their children's salvation by having them baptized before they have truly responded. Whatever the origin(s) of this

---

[6] Matthew Brady, "Southwestern Professor Says Baptists Losing Distinctive Principles," *Baptist Press* (September 10, 1991).

[7] Bob Allen, "Seminary President Says Southern Baptists Drifting Toward Infant Baptism," Baptist News Global (May 6, 2015), https://baptistnews.com/article/seminary-president-says-southern-baptists-drifting-toward-infant-baptism/.

phenomenon, there is a definite and troubling trend. And this trend is creating problems.

In my own evangelistic endeavors, I have found that sometimes the biggest obstacle to overcome in conversing with a lost person is that many obviously unregenerate people were baptized as infants or children. They assume their salvation is already certain because their parents had them baptized or their church baptized them at too young an age. I also often find myself counseling adults in the church who admit that they cannot clearly identify whether they are true Christians. Often, they point to a rushed experience of baptism as a child. Quite recently, a Southern Baptist pastor contacted me to help him work through his own questions about his salvation and his baptism.

How then shall we respond to the existence of these problems even as we seek to fulfill the biblical mandates for both child outreach and baptismal faithfulness? We are responsible, on the one hand, for introducing children to the Lord and, on the other hand, for baptizing those who have truly believed in the Lord, helping them to make proper confessions of their own personal faith. Neither the mandate for child evangelism nor the mandate for proper baptism may be surrendered. But how do we fulfill both divine mandates properly?

Toward the Proper Practice of Child Baptism

In my exercises of personal evangelism and of pastoral oversight over baptismal candidates, I have had the great privilege of engaging personally with numerous children. I am always reminded that every child is made in God's image and is unique as a human being. As a counselor, I must get on that child's personal level and speak to him or her face-to-face. I must then listen carefully to that child's answers, assiduously watching body language as well as vigilantly hearing vocal responses. I am reminded that God will hold those of us who are teachers to a higher account. The weight of that responsibility ought to rest heavily on the true shepherd's conscience (John 21:15–19).

Another writer in this volume was tasked with addressing child conversion, and the reader should consult that chapter. In the remainder of this chapter, I will focus instead on a practice I have found helpful as a pastor of children who are considering baptism—the baptismal counseling session. In general, with each person, and especially with children, I have found that it is necessary to have a dedicated counseling session. In these sessions, one must encourage gently, speak clearly, listen carefully, and ask appropriate questions.

Similarly, evangelistic presentations, such as those given during Vacation Bible School, should speak clearly at the child's level of cognition.[8] They should also be compelling without being overly emotional. Moreover, baptism should be offered only upon clear evidence of regeneration as the child makes his or her own personal confession. But how can we best arrive at knowing that a child has truly been converted? The baptism counseling session is key to moving forward responsibly with child baptism.

Schedule a meeting with a child who has indicated interest in being baptized. Providential wisdom given to a pastor asking an appropriate question kept me from making a hasty profession. During a counseling session, with my parents present, the pastor asked me about salvation. I was an intelligent seven-year-old and

---

[8] I praise the Lord personally that he saved me through the witness of a Vacation Bible School teacher!

provided adequate conceptual answers. However, I did not properly know my own sin. One of his questions opened my eyes to my need to confess my sin to God, which I did as I came to my baptism. I am very thankful for that probing question, for it led to a wrestling with God that prompted my true conversion and made my baptism as a child true rather than false. Following are some questions to ask a child during your conversation.

Questions to Ask a Child During a Baptismal Counseling Session

Please make an appointment with the child who is requesting baptism and make sure to include his or her parent(s). During the counseling session, it is first important to confirm, to the best of your ability, that a child understands that he or she is a sinner in need of a Savior. On this point, please read carefuly chapter 4 of this book, "Evangelism and Children," specifically the sections on "The Understanding of a Child" (p. 72) and "Communication with Children" (p. 75). After allowing a child to tell about his or her decision to accept Jesus as his or her Savior, consider the following questions for the child about baptism.

1. Tell me what baptism is. Is it something you think you are ready to do? Why do you want to be baptized? (Allow a child the freedom to express any anxieties about being in the water or being in front of a lot of people, then help address each concern.)
2. What does a person's baptism show? Sometimes it is helpful to explain to children that baptism is a way to show others what we believe about Jesus. Illustrate with the hand motions of baptism that going down into the baptismal waters then

coming back up is a way to tell others that one believes that Jesus died for our sins, was buried, then rose again.

A trip to your church's baptistery and getting-ready areas may help answer some of the child's questions. A "dry run" of showing the child how the pastor will lower the child in the water and bring him or her back up may help answer questions about what will happen during the baptism.

If a child does not feel ready for baptism, then pray with the child at the conclusion of your meeting for him or her to know when he or she is ready to let other people know about his or her decision for Christ.

Final Steps

Remind the child and parents of the basics of the Christian life, such as obeying God's Word, praying, reading the Bible regularly, attending worship regularly, bearing witness to Christ, and loving other people. Before the child and his or her parent(s) depart, have a word of prayer with the child, thanking God for how he is working in the child's life. (Pray this even if the child is not ready for baptism.)

Moreover, make sure the child is incorporated into a life group or Sunday school class, putting the child and parent(s) into contact with the responsible teacher. Then plan a follow-up session a few weeks after the baptism to see how the child's Christian life is progressing.

Finally, become a regular part of the child's life, looking into the progress of his or her spirituality. Enjoy seeing what God does in and through his precious children. And do not be surprised at the great things God does in and through those children's lives as they grow into mature Christians. I have seen this happen repeatedly with my own children and with many others. Jesus wants to bless the children through us, so let us do this and do it well!

Discussion Questions

1. What does it mean to receive the kingdom of God like a little child?
2. Describe water baptism and Spirit baptism.
3. What is the difference between personal knowledge and personal consent?
4. What questions or topics might you add to the twelve questions included here to ask a child during a baptismal counseling session?

Opportunities for Application

- Provide a new Christians class for children and their parents. Explain the responsibilities of believers, including baptism. Take a field trip to the baptistry and answer any questions.
- Provide a Scripture study and training session for those in your church who counsel children who are interested in becoming Christians or who have already made decisions for Christ.
- Some children need help understanding becoming a Christian and being baptized are two different events. Consider training leaders on how to talk to children about the purpose and symbol of baptism.

CHAPTER 7

A Theology of Children and the Church

David S. Dockery

The purpose of this important book on children and salvation is to explore wide-ranging questions regarding children's ministry. The goal of this chapter is to look carefully at issues related to church and church membership, with children and ministry to children in mind. We will seek to do so by engaging the meaning of church and church membership, including participation in the ordinances and the life of the church. Our exploration will be based on reflections from the teaching of the NT and practices of the people of God within the believers' church tradition. After offering reflections related to the church, we will explore applications for these truths as they relate to children and children's ministry.

The Church

The church is the community of people who have responded to God's gracious offer of salvation through faith in Jesus Christ. The church provides order, organization, and mission directives for the people of God. As far as is humanly possible, all believers in Christ are to involve themselves in his visible and organized church. A prerequisite for such involvement rests on being rightly related to God through Jesus Christ by grace through faith.[1]

It is acceptable in the English language to use the word "church" to mean a particular place where believers gather. It is also appropriate to use the term to describe the spiritual or universal church, which includes all the people of God on the earth at any one time together with all believers in Christ through the ages in heaven and on earth. "Church" is also used to describe certain denominations (e.g., the Lutheran Church) or the members of a state or national church (e.g., the Church of England) or believers in a particular area (e.g., the global church).

The church was inaugurated at Pentecost (Acts 2) as God's new society (Eph 2:15), which was built on the apostles and prophets

---

[1] For further insight regarding the meaning of the church in the believers' church tradition, see Gregg Allison, *Sojourners and Strangers: The Doctrine of the Church* (Crossway, 2012); C. Ryan Fields, *Local and Universal: A Free Church Account of Ecclesial Catholicity* (IVP, 2024); Earl D. Radmacher, *The Nature of the Church* (Western Seminary Press, 1972); Robert L. Saucy, *The Church in God's Program* (Moody, 1972); David S. Dockery, "God's Church: The Nature and Mission of the Church," in *Holman Bible Handbook*, ed. David S. Dockery (Holman, 1992); George Huntston Williams, "The Believers' Church and the Given Church," in *People of God: Essays on the Believers' Church*, ed. Paul Basden and David S. Dockery (Broadman, 1991).

(vv. 19–20) with Christ Jesus as the cornerstone (v. 21). The church belongs to God, who brought it into existence through Jesus Christ, his Son, and is enabled by the work of the Holy Spirit. Thus, it is vital to remember that the church is not primarily a human gathering but rather is a divinely created entity of the triune God.[2]

The Greek term *ekklēsia*, as used in the NT, is most often a reference to believers in Christ, being translated "church" in almost all English translations. The basic meaning of the term, however, is a gathering or an assembly, such as the unruly mob in Acts 19:32 or the lawful assembly in Acts 19:39. First Thessalonians 1:1 is a reference to a church in a particular place, while Gal 1:22 points to a group of churches across a geographic region. The apostle Paul also used the term to look beyond local churches to the universal church in passages like Eph 1:22–23 and Col 1:22–23. Our discussion recognizes the distinction between the local church and the universal church in the believers' church tradition. Of the 114 usages of *ekklēsia*, the large majority point to a local church in a particular place or context, so this usage will be prioritized in our chapter.[3]

The church is pictured in the NT in multiple ways, but one in particular connects closely with the emphasis of this book. The church is portrayed as a family or household. The members of the church, who have been redeemed by the blood of Jesus Christ, are God's children (Gal 4:1–7), with Jesus Christ as the firstborn of the family (Rom 8:29). The theme of family is prominent in the Pastoral

---

[2] F. P. Cotterell, "Church," in *New Dictionary of Theology*, ed. Sinclair B. Ferguson et al. (IVP, 1988), 140–43.

[3] See Fields, *Local and Universal;* Williams, "The Believers' Church and the Given Church."

Epistles, where the church is described as "God's household, . . . the pillar and foundation of the truth" (1 Tim 3:15).[4]

Church Membership and the Ordinances

Membership in this family or household is conditional on declaration of one's personal faith in Jesus Christ, expressed in the NT through the practice of believer's baptism. The NT maintains that faith is the means by which believing people receive the salvation purchased by the cross work of the Lord Jesus Christ (Eph 2:8–9). Faith includes a commitment of the whole person to the Lord Jesus, a commitment that involves both knowledge and trust, which is evidenced by obedience and good works. Faith is not merely an intellectual assent or an emotional response: it is an inward spiritual change enabled and confirmed by the Holy Spirit.[5]

Conversion, then, involves more than intellectual assent, but it includes knowledge and understanding about Christ. The object of faith, however, is not primarily the teaching about Christ but Jesus Christ himself. In our belief in and commitment to Jesus Christ, we acknowledge him as Savior from sin and Lord of our lives, even Lord of all creation (Rom 10:9). Genuine conversion involves a belief in Jesus Christ as the God-man, and in his work as Redeemer. Assent to orthodox doctrine, as important as it may be, is not enough in itself for salvation, which calls for a living faith and trust in Jesus Christ. A foundational understanding among NT believers is that the Spirit of God enables people to truly understand the gospel and to authentically trust

---

[4] See Paul S. Minear, *Images of the Church in the New Testament* (WJK, 2004).

[5] James Leo Garrett, *Systematic Theology: Biblical, Historical, and Evangelical*, 2 vols. (Eerdmans, 1995), 2:534–35.

in Christ. All of these believers are given the gift of God's Spirit, for no one can confess Jesus as Lord except by the Holy Spirit (1 Cor 12:3).[6]

This confession is made public though baptism, a practice commanded by the resurrected Christ (Matt 28:19–20). In the book of Acts, baptism is associated with faith and repentance as a qualification of membership in the church (2:37–42). Baptism served the function of not only initiation into the church but also an identification with the crucified and risen Christ, providing a sign of covenant relationship with Christ and his people (Rom 6:1–4; Col 2:9–13).[7]

Baptism is the initiation act whereby one is made a member of the church, identifying with Christ and his people. The act of baptism is not restricted to any group or class of people; its only restriction is an expression of genuine faith (Gal 3:27–28; 1 Cor 12:13). The NT does not know of believers who have not been baptized (Acts 2:41). Baptism signifies burial with Christ in his death as well as new life, a life shared with Christ's risen life. The act of baptism is a valuable teaching medium for new believers and the entire church. Every time a new believer is baptized, the symbolic meaning of baptism is to be communicated to boys, girls, men, and women.[8] With this understanding, we can now define a local church as a group of baptized believers banded and covenanted together for worship, edification, service, fellowship, and outreach, accepting spiritual leadership, willing to minister to and serve all segments of society (including

---

[6] Charles L. Quarles, "Explaining the Gospel to Kids," in *The Mission of Today's Church: Baptist Leaders Look at Modern Faith Issues*, ed. R. Stanton Norman (B&H Academic, 2007).

[7] David S. Dockery, "Baptism I: Gospels," in *IVP Dictionary of the New Testament: A One-Volume Compendium of Contemporary Biblical Scholarship*, ed. Daniel G. Reid (IVP, 2004), 96–99.

[8] David S. Dockery, "A Theology of Baptism," *SWJT* 43 (Spring 2001): 4–16.

children) through the various spiritual gifts in the body of Christ, and regularly practicing the ordinances.[9]

In addition to baptism, the church has a second ordinance, which is the Lord's Supper. While baptism is a one-time act picturing the believer's new identification with Christ and his people, the Lord's Supper is to be practiced on a regular basis for the remaining years of the believer's life on this earth. When the church celebrates the Supper, it does so to remember the broken body and shed blood of Jesus Christ. The Lord's Supper is a sermon in silence, proclaiming Christ through the symbols of the bread and the cup. The elements of the Supper take believers back to the scenes of redemption, not in some nostalgic manner but in a vivid reminder of the One who died, was raised, and who is coming again.

The celebration of the Supper is central to the church's worship and thus should be a regular occurrence in the life of the church (Acts 20:7; 1 Cor 11:17–24). Only those who have placed their faith in Jesus Christ and who are members of the body of Christ are invited to partake of the Lord's Supper. Believers are gathered in one sacred and joyful celebration following apostolic teaching and practice. Indeed, in the observance of this ordinance, the whole of what Christianity means is expressed: one Lord Jesus Christ, incarnate, atoning, and triumphant as the sum and substance of the Supper. The essential meaning of the ordinance can certainly be grasped by a child, but the depth of its meaning will never be fully understood this side of eternity.[10]

---

[9] David S. Dockery, "A Pauline Theology of the Church," in *The Community of Jesus: A Theology of the Church*, ed. Christopher Morgan and Ken Easley (B&H Academic, 2013).

[10] David S. Dockery, "The Church, Worship, and the Lord's Supper," in *The Mission of Today's Church: Baptist Leaders Look at Modern Faith Issues*, ed. R. Stanton Norman (B&H Academic, 2007), 37–50.

The Meaning of Membership

At the time of salvation, believers are called into fellowship with Jesus Christ (1 John 1:3) and then brought into fellowship with other believers, who share life together in the body of Christ. This fellowship constitutes the first step of membership in the church of the Lord Jesus Christ (1 Cor 1:9).[11] Membership in the church is both doxological and missiological, as well as confessional and covenantal. Believers are called to doxology, that is, to worship, praise, adore, and love the triune God, and to mission, that is, to share the gospel message and serve others for the sake of Christ. On this point, there is wide agreement. But let us delve a bit further into the confessional and covenantal markers.[12]

One enters the church by confessing that Jesus is Lord (Rom 10:9; 1 Cor 12:3). Church membership has historically involved not only this personal confession but also a confession of the basic tenets of the historic Christian faith. Members confess their faith before God and before their fellow human beings, committing themselves to the doctrine, ethics, and practices of a specific church. Some churches adopt a particular doctrinal statement, which they may use to instruct or catechize members.

In addition to its confessional nature, those in the believers' church tradition have frequently emphasized the covenantal nature of church membership, which stresses not only a relationship with God but one also with other followers of Christ.[13] Two markers frame the

---

[11] Saucy, *The Church in God's Program*, 100–04.

[12] Allison, *Sojourners and Strangers*, 123–40.

[13] See Charles Deweese, *Baptist Church Covenants* (Broadman, 1990); Paul Fiddes, *Baptists and the Communion of Saints: A Theology of Covenanted Disciples* (Baylor University Press, 2014); Travis Trawick, "The Regenerate,

covenantal relationship: (1) baptism serves as a one-time initiation marker into the new covenant, and (2) the practice of Lord's Supper provides an ongoing reminder of participation in the new covenant (1 Cor 11:25; 2 Cor 3:6).

A covenantal framework is used to identify the commitments that members make to God and to one another related to shared worship, regular attendance, participation in the ordinances, lifestyle expectations, and care for one another. Gregg Allison suggests, "The covenantal framework of the church that should regulate the relationships between its members is built into the fabric of the New Testament."[14] Stanley Grenz insightfully stressed the combination of the confessional and covenantal aspects of church membership, noting that the "mutual confession of Jesus as the Christ means that the members are conscious of their special standing in fellowship with each other; their shared commitment to be disciples of the Lord entails a commitment to one another. The church-constituting covenant is a mutual agreement to walk together as the people of God."[15] Connected with these practices, some churches emphasize the background, principles, and service or ministry expectations of their members. Membership opens the door and serves as an invitation to participate in all aspects of the life and work of the church.

Both the confession and the covenant remind us of the importance of a church's regenerate membership. Membership includes only the regenerate, but it is open to all the truly regenerate regardless of age, sex, ethnicity, marital status, nationality, educational level,

---

Gathered, Baptized Congregation of Christ: A Theology of Church Covenant" (PhD diss., SWBTS, 2021).

[14] Allison, *Sojourners and Strangers,* 125.

[15] Stanley J. Grenz, *Theology for the Community of God* (Eerdmans, 1994), 613–14.

or socio-economic level (1 Cor 12:13; Gal 3:28; Eph 5:22–6:9; Col 3:11). Participation in the membership of the church, like other practices, is to be done decently and in order (1 Cor 14:40). Members worship with one another, care for one another, and serve one another by exercising their spiritual gifts, functioning as a spiritual priesthood in obedience to Christ (Matt 28:20; Rom 12:9–21; 1 Cor 12:14; Eph 4:11–16; 1 Pet 2:5–9; 4:10–11). Members commit themselves to the unity of the church, manifesting the fruit of the Spirit and making every effort to keep the unity of the Spirit through the bond of peace (Gal 5:22–23; Eph 4:1–6). Members accept spiritual oversight and instruction, admonishing and warning one another for the good of the body (1 Thess 5:12–14; Titus 1:9). Members care for those in need, including little ones, the least of these, and the lost (Matt 25:40; Jas 1:27). Members teach one another the truths of the Christian faith and work together to take the gospel of Jesus Christ to those in their area, in this country, and across the globe, to "make disciples of all nations" (Matt 28:19), doing all of these things for the good of the church, the advancement of the gospel, and the glory of God (1 Cor 10:31).[16]

Children and Church Membership

Reflecting on this overview of the basics of the NT teaching regarding the church, we must ask a foundational question: Can children be members of a local church? The question has been answered differently by various groups during different periods of church history. Before addressing this important question, we must make sure that

[16] See Dockery, "A Pauline Theology for the Church;" also, David S. Dockery, "A Theology for the Church," in *Midwestern Journal of Theology* 1, no. 1 (2003): 10–20.

we have answered a more foundational question related to children and salvation.[17]

While children may not be able to grasp the depth regarding all of the marvelous truths associated with atonement, redemption, and justification, they are quite able to understand that God has created them in his image (Gen 1:26–27); that he loves them (Rom 5:6, 8); that they are sinners who have fallen short of God's expectations (3:23); that Jesus Christ lived a perfect life and died a vicarious death that provided forgiveness for our sins (1 Pet 3:18); and that, on the third day, he was victoriously raised from the dead (1 Cor 15:3–4). They certainly can share in the hope of eternal life (John 3:16). I have often said to people that while my parents were not theologians, they taught me basic truths in my childhood that have guided my life for many decades, including that God is love (1 John 4:8), that the Bible is true (2 Tim 3:16), and that Jesus saves (Luke 19:10). Thanks be to God that with the enablement of the Holy Spirit, I have grown and matured in my understanding of these truths. My deepening in them, however, has never meant outgrowing these essential faith commitments.

Those called to serve in children's ministry need to work with parents and teachers to help introduce children to the meaning of these faith commitments.[18] They can guide children to recognize that Jesus Christ is himself God. In addition, by entering the world as a human (John 1:14), Jesus took on a human nature and

---

[17] See Roy B. Zuck, *Precious in His Sight: Childhood and Children of the Bible* (Wipf & Stock, 2012).

[18] See Lawrence O. Richards, *Children's Ministry: Nurturing Faith Within the Family of God* (Zondervan, 1988); Robert E. Clark et al., *Childhood Education in the Church* (Moody, 1986).

human characteristics while voluntarily choosing to exercise his divine powers only intermittently to fulfill the redemptive mission he came to this earth to accomplish. While Jesus identified completely with fallen humanity, the Bible is equally clear in confessing his sinlessness (Rom 8:3; Heb 4:15). The Bible stresses the true emptying of Jesus to become like us (Phil 2:5–8) and thus declares his full humanity, including the reality of the temptations, his Spirit-enabled rejection of those temptations (Matt 4:1–11), and his resulting sinlessness.

Children can grasp the essential truth that Jesus came to this earth to be the Savior of the world (John 4:42). Jesus possessed inwardly and demonstrated outwardly the very nature of God himself (Col 1:15–16; 2:9; Heb 1:2–3). While the great mystery of the incarnation is something on which we all continue to meditate and about which we seek to develop in our understanding, it is necessary for believers of any age to acknowledge that Christ is both God and man. Only as a man could he be the Redeemer for boys, girls, men, and women; and only as a sinless man could he fittingly die for others. Only as God could his life, ministry, and redeeming death have infinite value. Children can grow in their understanding of these truths as they mature in the grace and knowledge of the Lord Jesus Christ, so that their faith in Christ and their worship of him are deepened and strengthened along the way.[19] He is indeed the "Jesus loves me" of the children's song and the "Holy, Holy, Holy" of the church's great hymn.

Children, with childlike faith, can believe that Jesus was raised from the dead and is now exalted at God's right hand. These truths

---

[19] See Quarles, "Explaining the Gospel to Kids," 59–72; also, Dennis Gunderson, *Your Child's Profession of Faith* (Calvary, 1994).

provide hope for victory over death as they watch the earthly life of their grandparents come to an end. Boys and girls, like men and women, can confess Jesus as Lord, our Prophet, Priest, and King, who has completely made God known (John 1:1, 14, 18) and who has brought peace between God and those of all ages who have placed their faith in him (Rom 5:1). In Christ, boys and girls as well as men and women express their belief, hope, and trust, offering heartfelt thanksgiving for the salvation he has provided for us.

Children can share with others that they have trusted in Christ by being baptized.[20] This should only be done after several thoughtful and careful conversations with the children in an effort to avoid superficial decisions. Parents, if at all possible, should be included in these vitally important conversations. We all recognize the tendency for children to want to do what they see others in their children's groups at church doing. We also recognize that children are at various stages of intellectual, emotional, and spiritual development (1 Cor 13:11). For these and other reasons, some in the believers' church tradition have urged churches to wait until children evidence certain levels of maturity in their lives, as they approach adulthood, before being baptized.

Yet, it needs to be stressed that while this chapter is about the theology of children and the church, boys and girls need not be mature theologians to genuinely confess their faith in Christ (Matt 18:1–6; Eph 6:1–2). Children who are able to provide a credible profession of their faith are also capable of participating in the church's ordinances and carrying out the basic responsibilities of church membership, including love and service of others. I believe we find guidance in

---

[20] William L. Hendricks, *A Theology for Children* (Broadman, 1980), 180–82.

this regard from the apostle Paul's letter to the Ephesians (especially Eph 1:1–2; 4:17–6:9).[21]

Paul's letter to the Ephesians has been praised throughout the centuries as one of the greatest and most relevant of Paul's works.[22] It is certainly the most majestic portrait in the NT of the church and the unity of God's people. The grand letter begins with Paul's self-identification (1:1). Initially, and important for the observations that follow, Ephesians probably was intended to be a circular letter, sent to other churches in addition to the one in Ephesus. This means that this inspired teaching had importance for churches beyond Ephesus in the first century and has significant implications for believers in our day as well. Still, we recognize that the most prominent recipients were the believers in Ephesus.[23]

Paul followed the custom of his day in his letters by identifying himself before noting to whom the letter was addressed. The letter was written to "saints," those in whom the Spirit of God had worked to bring salvation. The term "saints" also functioned as a synonym for the members of the believing community. Saints are holy ones, people who have been called and set apart in Christ. All persons who have repented of their sins and who have placed their hope and faith in Christ are saints. To these saints, Paul offered a greeting of "grace and peace" (vv. 1–2 NIV).

Central to the message of Ephesians is the re-creation of God's redeemed family according to his original intention for humanity at

---

[21] See Walter L. Liefeld, *Ephesians*, IVP New Testament Commentary Series (IVP, 1997), 29–31.

[22] See John A Mackay, *God's Order: The Ephesian Letter and This Present Time* (Macmillan, 1964), x.

[23] See David S. Dockery, "The Pauline Epistles," in *Holman Illustrated Bible Handbook*, ed. Steve Bond and Jeremy Howard (B&H, 2013).

the time of creation (3:14–21). The new creation destroyed the misguided view that God accepted the Jews and rejected the Gentiles (2:11–19). Paul claimed that this distinction was abolished at Christ's sacrificial death. Thus, no more hindrance remains for reuniting all humanity as God's people with Christ as Head (1:22–23). God has endowed the new body, the church, with the Holy Spirit's power. He has done so to enable the members to live out their new lives (1:3–3:21) and to put into practice the new standards of the Christian covenantal community (4:1–6:20).[24] In summary, the overall emphasis of Ephesians is the church's unity in Christ through the power of the Holy Spirit.[25]

In the second half of the letter, the apostle identified some of the key groups in the church, all of whom are included in the "saints" to whom the letter was addressed. It has been noted that this section represents the guidelines for the new covenant in general and for each individual member of the new humanity.[26] The church should not be characterized by falsehood, sinful rage, stealing, corrupt words, or mean-spiritedness. Instead, believers are to be kind, to speak truth in love, to work hard, and to participate in gracious and edifying conversations, forgiving one another as God in Christ Jesus has forgiven those who have trusted in Christ (4:17–32). Moreover, these saints are to be imitators of God in showing love and kindness to others and in reflecting God's goodness to those in the church and in the fallen world (5:1–17).

---

[24] See David S. Dockery, *Ephesians: One Body in Christ* (Lifeway, 1996).

[25] David S. Dockery, "An Exposition of Ephesians 4:1–6," *Review and Expositor* 88 (1991): 79–82.

[26] Peter Gentry, "Speaking the Truth in Love (Eph 4:15): Life in the New Covenant Community," *SBJT* 10, no. 2 (Summer 2006): 70–72.

In Eph 5:18–21, Paul exhorted the saints to "be filled by the Spirit." The Spirit's fullness is demonstrated in spiritual insight, praise, and thanksgiving that are constant and comprehensive. The church that is filled with the Spirit will be characterized by praise and thanksgiving to God and will also exhibit evidence of self-control, upbuilding fellowship, and mutual submission. The apostle then applied these truths to wives and husbands (vv. 22–33), children and parents (6:1–4), and masters and servants (vv. 5–9).[27]

Let us look at Paul's wise words in Eph 6:1–4. Interestingly, Paul followed the guidelines of the ethical teaching of his day by focusing on children first, but Paul went beyond these teachings, offering a reciprocal word for parents. The point is that both children and parents are to hear Paul's instructions. It seems clear that Paul's address to the children indicates that he anticipated they would be present in the church meeting when the letter was initially read, implying at least that Paul assumed the context of believing families. A healthy respect for authority provides the framework and the foundation for Paul to offer this twofold word to children: obey and honor.[28]

Parents have the responsibility both to discipline and to instruct their children. One of the goals of child-rearing is for parents to help children come to the place of accepting God's rule in their lives in a real and personal way through discipline and instruction. To bring this about, parents need to recognize that children are gifts from

---

[27] Dockery, *Ephesians*, 104–9; Bob Gonzalez, "Children, Church Membership, and the Implications of Ephesians 6:1," Sharper Iron, July 16, 2019, https://sharperiron.org/article/children-church-membership-and-implications-of-ephesians-61.

[28] Harold W. Hoehner, *Ephesians: An Exegetical Commentary* (Baker, 2002), 785–91.

God (Ps 127:4–5). Understood within this broader context, children in the believing community at Ephesus (Eph 6:1) are to be recognized as saints (1:1), who are to be filled with the Spirit (5:18), putting their faith into practice in the fear of Christ (5:21).

The word for children (*tekna*) is broad enough to refer to minors, including older children in the stage of adolescence, but certainly not adults. While we cannot know for sure the age of the children being addressed, Paul does assume that the recipients of the letter could understand the directive. These *tekna* were not adults. Those who would suggest that baptism, church membership, and participation in the Lord's Supper should be reserved for adults seem counter to Paul's approach in Ephesians.

While we cannot put an age limit on baptism, church membership (including voting privileges), and Lord's Supper participation, we recognize that some aspects of church membership, especially leadership roles, need to be reserved for adults. We can affirm that all regenerate members, including children, may participate in worship, singing, fellowship, prayer, listening to preaching, learning from teaching, caring for others, and other opportunities of service. If and when needed, children will also from time to time be recipients of correction and pastoral care.[29]

If the Lord brings children to faith in Christ and if salvation is prerequisite for baptism, church membership, and Lord's Supper participation, then baptism, church membership, and Lord's Supper participation should be open to children as well as adults. It would seem that, for the sake of consistency, churches should not baptize children unless they are willing to grant church membership to them and invite them to the Lord's Table.

---

[29] Hendricks, *A Theology for Children*, 180–87.

Guidance for Children, Parents, and Those Serving in Children's Ministry

The first application of these observations is directed toward parents and those serving in children's ministry, flowing as an extension from the Ephesians 6 passage to help children come to a place of accepting God's rule in their lives (vv. 3–4).[30] Children need love, significance, and security as well as tender instruction, the goal of which is to help establish boundaries and guidelines for children. Proverbs 22:6 offers a wise word in guiding children to become obedient and godly in whatever God-honoring direction their lives may take.

Neither the apostle Paul's words nor any other words in Scripture encourage us to force children into a preconceived mold. The responsibility of parents and those called to serve in children's ministry, at formal times and informal times, is to instruct them in God's ways so that their lives can be holy and pleasing in God's sight. The instructions in Deut 6:6–7 remain applicable as we look for formal times of instruction, designated times for reading, and scheduled times for doing things together with the children. Informal times are also exceedingly valuable opportunities with children. We recognize that often more is caught than taught. Children hear what is said and observe what takes place, calling for all of us to speak encouraging, upbuilding, and healing words.

These biblical principles are unchanging, but changing circumstances may call for more reflective and focused application. As with Timothy, who learned from his mother and his grandmother (2 Tim 1:5), instruction in the Scriptures and application of the

---

[30] Clinton E. Arnold, *Ephesians*, Exegetical Commentary on the New Testament (Zondervan, 2010), 417–19.

biblical teaching should begin at an early age, even before children are ready to turn their hearts to Christ and identify with him in baptism. The church must be sure that all ministry to children grows out of solid scriptural foundation, even as those in children's ministry adapt to the needs of children and new models of learning connected with technology.

What has traditionally been called Sunday school or Bible study remains a key piece for the church's ministry to children, but other small group initiatives and family learning models need to be explored. Each church must think carefully regarding the presence of children during the time of worship. Some churches will encourage this practice and have children sit together with their families. Such practices need accompanying activities to help children understand the meaning of the songs that are sung and the message that is preached. Parents will need resources to guide their efforts to be parents in the pews, leading their families in worship together during the services.

Some churches may opt for children's worship while others may choose to allow children to be present for a portion of the church's worship service and then be dismissed before the sermon. Many congregations will want to augment these efforts with missions-focused programs and Scripture-memory initiatives, along with children's choirs, Vacation Bible School, summer camps, and other special activities designed to train and strengthen the spiritual formation of children. We pray that such efforts would bear much fruit and lead to the development of willing hearts among children to serve and exercise the gifts that the Lord has given to them.[31]

---

[31] See Robert J. Choun, "Children's Ministry Models," in *Evangelical Dictionary of Christian Education*, ed. Michael J. Anthony (Baker, 2001), 128–29.

As noted earlier, the role of catechisms should not be ignored. This practice has been actively observed in the believers' church tradition since the seventeenth century. The practice can be traced through Benjamin Keach (1640–1704), Charles Spurgeon (1834–1892), and John Broadus (1827–1895), whose catechism for children was a foundational publication for the Baptist Sunday School Board in 1891.[32] Derived from the Greek word *katechē*, meaning "to make hear" or "to instruct," catechistic practices can be traced back to the earliest centuries of the church and have been an aspect of instruction for children (and adults as well) in every Christian tradition.[33]

The practice was especially prominent during the time of the Reformation in the sixteenth century. Following the patterns found in the Apostle's Creed and the Didache (a second-century document to pass along the teaching associated with the apostolic tradition), catechistic instruction has been used to prioritize the essential truths of the Christian faith that Christ followers and church members of all ages need to know. Churches need to consider ways to adopt catechistic instruction in our day to strengthen the biblical and theological understanding of children, as well as of parents and those who serve in children's ministry. Doing so in association with baptism, church membership, and participation in the Lord's Supper would be a step toward healthier congregations and stronger families and would strengthen young disciples

---

[32] Thomas J. Nettles, *Teaching Truth, Training Hearts: The Study of Catechisms in Baptist Life* (Calvary, 1998); also, see Jonathan Watson, "The Relationship Between Baptism, Catechesis, and Entrance to the Church: An Argument for a Theological Catalyst" (PhD diss., SWBTS, 2015).

[33] See Michael Dujarier, *A History of the Catechumenate: The First Six Centuries*, trans. Edward J. Haasl (William H. Sadler, 1979).

to follow Christ faithfully and obediently for the remainder of their lives.[34]

Churches in the rapidly changing world of the twenty-first century must rethink and reprioritize ministry to children, providing thoughtful and insightful approaches to the place of children in the church and the importance of children's education, to begin to form and inform their understanding of the essentials of church membership and involvement. The goal is not merely additional programs and activities but the development of scripturally grounded and theologically informed approaches to reach children with the gospel message of Jesus Christ and to form lifelong followers of Christ who will love the triune God with all of their hearts and minds, even as they develop a growing commitment to the written Word of God and to the people of God, all for the glory of God.

Discussion Questions

1. Discuss your church's policy for membership. Are there any age restrictions?
2. What are some ways children can serve others in the local church?
3. How are children included on a regular basis in your church's worship-service ministry opportunities? What would you like to see added or revised based on your reading of this chapter?

---

[34] See Dale Moody, "Baptism in Theology and Practice," in *People of God: Essays on the Believers' Church*, ed. Paul Basden and David S. Dockery (Broadman, 1991); Millard J. Erickson, "The Lord's Supper," in *People of God: Essays on the Believers' Church*, ed. Paul Basden and David S. Dockery (Broadman, 1991).

4. Which verse(s) mentioned in this chapter challenged and/ or reinforced your current beliefs about children and church membership?

Opportunities for Application

- Consider training a small group of people to specifically counsel children who express a desire to become Christians or be baptized. Plan to have at least one person from that group available at each of your church's worship services if your pastor gives an invitation to make a decision for Christ at the end of worship services.
- Consider establishing a new members class designed specifically for children where they can learn about their responsibilities and privileges as church members as described in this chapter. Plan to include learning activities related to church ordinances and spiritual disciplines.
- Consider providing opportunities for children to participate in corporate worship. Whether through singing, reading Scripture, leading a prayer, following along with a children's bulletin, or giving offerings, there are many visible or tangible ways for children to actively participate in weekly services.
- Formalize your church's policies on child safety in your church building and programs. Enlist a team or committee to regularly address ongoing needs for policy updates and to assure implementation is consistent and nonnegotiable.

CHAPTER 8

The Urgency of Child Discipleship

Shelly Melia

Returning to his friend's home after conducting meetings in a town in England, D. L. Moody was asked by his host, "How many were converted tonight in the meeting?"

"Two and a half," replied Moody.

"What do you mean?" asked his friend. "Were there two adults and a child?"

"No," said the evangelist, "it was two children and an adult. The children have given their lives to Christ in their youth, while the adult has come with half of his life."[1]

When children respond to the gospel, they are blessed with a lifetime of opportunities for growth and discipleship.

[1] This is a familiar story passed down about D. L. Moody. The source for this version is Lois E. LeBar, *Children in the Bible School: The* How *of Christian Education* (Fleming H. Revell, 1962), 26–27.

Charles Spurgeon, a well-known preacher during the nineteenth century, echoed Moody's view of children: "Capacity for believing lies more in the child than in the man. We grow less rather than more capable of faith: every year brings the unregenerate mind further away from God."[2] However, there is a difference between acknowledging a child's capacity for discipleship and intentionally stewarding that capacity well. "Discipleship is not passive. It requires work and usually involves believers speaking into the lives of less mature Christ followers."[3] The goal of child discipleship is to teach children how to follow Jesus for their whole lives. This chapter will address the urgent need to evaluate current practices and will focus on four key essentials of child discipleship.

Acknowledge the Progress

There was a time in Baptist churches when a child would walk an aisle in response to a public invitation, sit on the front row to fill out a decision form, be presented to the congregation, and then be placed in a handshake and hug line at the end of the service. While the work of the Holy Spirit was not inhibited or limited by this approach, most churches have adopted more intentional practices when it comes to a child's decision to follow Christ. A commitment to individual counseling and involvement from parents is now more commonly found

---

[2] Charles Haddon Spurgeon, "Jesus and the Children," in *Metropolitan Tabernacle Pulpit*, vol. 32, The Spurgeon Center for Biblical Preaching at Midwestern Seminary, https://www.spurgeon.org/resource-library/sermons/jesus-and-the-children/#flipbook/.

[3] Ken Hindman et al., *Every Age Every Stage: Teaching God's Truth at Home and Church* (B&H, 2021), 8.

in churches. And, for some churches, a meeting with a minister is a prerequisite for baptism, and completion of a new Christians class is required for church membership. Clearly, there has been progress in how children are guided and counseled when they make the decision to follow Christ.

While there has been progress in how ministries process the salvation event with children, there is a need for more attention and focus on what is done with children to foster a deep and lasting faith. For example, many children respond to the gospel at large events like Vacation Bible School or children's camp. All hands are on deck for those evangelistic opportunities, and there is often training for counselors who will talk with the children who respond. The breakdown occurs after the child works through the process the church has in place to counsel and prepare the child for baptism. It is as if a collective sigh of relief is breathed when the child is baptized because there is tangible and measurable evidence for the child's decision. Baptism can be mistakenly viewed as the finish line, and the need to disciple children is often not emphasized.

Review Foundational Principles

Before focusing on the need to increase the priority placed on child discipleship, take a moment to review these foundational principles about children and salvation:

- There is no specific pattern for children and salvation found in the Bible.
- Jesus said, "Let the little children come to me" (Mark 10:14).
- Children can respond to the gospel, and churches need to think carefully about how to best shepherd them.

- There is no set age at which children are universally ready to be saved. (See Harwood's chapter in this book.)
- Respect the work of the Holy Spirit in the salvation of a child. The Holy Spirit draws the child, and a reliance on the Holy Spirit requires sensitivity on the part of the minister or parent.
- There must be an understanding of the child's capacities without overrating them or underrating them.[4] There is a tendency to swing too far to one side or the other. On the one hand, some may underestimate the ability of a child to believe and respond to the gospel. In this case, children may be discouraged from making decisions or pushed aside as too young. On the other hand, some may overestimate a child's understanding of salvation and rush the child into baptism without taking time to talk with the child about his or her decision.

Finding the right balance in approaching children and salvation can be challenging. The review of these foundational principles is not meant to cast doubt in the minds of those who desire to lead children to Christ. Rather, the intention is to help ministers and parents recognize their dependence on the Holy Spirit to do his work and to expand our thinking about the ways in which children are shepherded. The event of salvation is not the only time there is a tendency to overrate or underrate the capacity of children. A child's decision is celebrated as the most important decision he will make in his life, but then the expectations of growth and formation do not match the magnitude of the decision.

---

[4] Eugene Chamberlain, *When Can a Child Believe?* (Broadman, 1973), 36.

In the best of circumstances, the Christian family will benefit from the influence of and participation in a community of faith that values and prioritizes faith formation in children.[5] The OT makes it clear that the nuclear family was important, but there was also a clear pattern of meaningful participation in a faith community. Catherine Stonehouse and Scottie May point out the following:

> In villages and tribes where such faith was lived, the teaching a child received at home would be reinforced and demonstrated in the life of the community. Families would gather with the whole community for annual feast to worship and reenact the story of what God had done for them (Deuteronomy 16:1–7).[6]

The Need for More Emphasis on Child Discipleship

What is the evidence for prioritizing child discipleship? According to Lifeway Research, only 23 percent of Americans attend church weekly, with 59 percent indicating they rarely or never attend church.[7] The statistics are even more alarming when it comes to the numbers of young adults walking away from their childhood faith. Jim Davis and Michael Graham refer to this as "dechurching." In their estimation, "dechurching" represents "the largest and fastest religious shift"

---

[5] This chapter does not focus on the importance of the family. Please see chapter 7 for a robust discussion on the role of the family in discipling children.

[6] Catherine Stonehouse and Scottie May, *Listening to Children on the Spiritual Journey* (Baker Academic, 2010), 123.

[7] Lifeway Research, "Fast Facts," Lifeway Christian Resources, https://research.lifeway.com/fast-facts/.

in American history, as tens of millions of adults who once attended church are no longer attending.[8] "Dechurching is an epidemic and will impact both the institutions of our country and the very fabric of our society within our lifetime."[9] In addition, a 2023 Gallup poll found that 75 percent of participants think religion is losing its influence on American life.[10] Considering these trends and beginning to create strategies for effective child discipleship is imperative for churches and parents.

In addition to the exodus of adults who once attended church, there is a growing need for young people to respond to a call to ministry. Decreasing enrollment in theological training programs and an increased need for churches to replace retiring ministers both point to the reality many churches face today as they struggle to staff key ministry positions. "Part of this decline may be traced to poor disciple making efforts of local churches."[11]

Declining church attendance, the prevalence of "dechurching," religion's decreasing influence in the world, and the reality of fewer young people stepping into ministry roles—all of this together only scratches the surface of a growing body of evidence exposing the need to reconsider the effectiveness of our child discipleship strategies. "The greatest challenge to the future of faith is the discipleship of our children."[12]

---

[8] Jim Davis and Michael Graham, *The Great Dechurching: Who's Leaving, Why Are They Going, and What Will It Take to Bring Them Back?* (Zondervan, 2023), 3.

[9] Davis and Graham, 7.

[10] "Religion," Gallup, https://news.gallup.com/poll/1690/Religion.aspx.

[11] J. D. Payne, "An Overlooked Reason for Decline in Seminary Enrollment," Church Leaders, July 21, 2023, https://www.jdpayne.org/2023/05/an-overlooked-reason-for-decline-in-seminary-enrollment/.

[12] Valerie Bell et al., *Resilient: Child Discipleship and the Fearless Future of the Church* (AWANA Clubs International, 2020), 33.

The secular world understands the value of gaining the young child's attention and devotion.

Unlimited access to digital devices allows opposing worldviews to penetrate and influence the developing hearts and minds of children and teens before their biblical worldview and faith are formed. In effect, children are being discipled by the virtual world while the real-world influence of their community of faith is dulled or muted.

What can be done to reverse these trends and reestablish the church and home as primary influencers in the lives of our children? It will take more than trendy programmatic changes in children's ministry to make child discipleship the priority. "Will we realize too late that we gave them things that didn't travel into their adult lives as anything more than spiritual entertainment and moralistic stories, things lacking real spiritual power and proactive purpose?"[13]

Shift Focus from Salvation as Transactional to Salvation as Transformational

In his seminal book, *Children and Conversion,* Clifford Ingle makes this statement: "The psychology of the United States is largely a pragmatic one based upon 'growth,' 'success,' and 'achievement'; so the churches themselves are caught up in the obsession for growth, success, and achievement."[14] Even though Ingle penned these words in 1970, the same words could be written about churches today. One way this mindset shows up is in the questions people ask children's ministers or pastors after evangelistic events: "How many children

[13] Bell, 35.

[14] Clifford Ingle, *Children and Conversion* (Broadman, 1970), 155.

came forward at Vacation Bible School?" "How many children were saved at camp?" These questions are not bad questions. They are questions that come from a desire to know and celebrate the good things that are happening.

However, if the only metric used for measuring the effectiveness of an event is the number of decisions made, the focus leans too heavily on the event of salvation, and more emphasis is needed on the process of transformation (discipleship) in a child's life. Decisions and baptisms are easy to count. Measuring the transformation of a child is much more difficult. While it may be impossible to measure spiritual transformation in real time, there is a need to take a long look at the effectiveness of discipleship rather than to rely solely on immediate results. Shifting focus toward salvation as transformational does not devalue or discount the event of salvation. Rather, it reminds churches, ministers, and parents of this important truth: "Christ's salvation is for the whole of life. He demands the whole of life from one he has saved. A child may easily get the impression that when he receives Christ his soul is saved quite apart from his body and his conduct."[15]

Refocus Efforts on Child Discipleship

Viewing salvation and child discipleship through the lens of transformation sets the bar much higher for both the family and the local church. Brian Dembowczyk, in *Family Discipleship That Works,* suggests children "like the *idea* of faith but are missing the *substance* of faith. Those who are rejecting the faith, then, aren't rejecting the

[15] Gaines S. Dobbins, *Winning the Children* (Broadman, 1953), 141.

gospel, but a caricature of the gospel. They are turning their backs on a mirage."[16] While the following principles relate to discipling children after salvation, they also apply to children still early in their journeys of faith formation.

Relationships Are Key

Relationships are essential to effective discipleship of children. Matt Markins, in his book, *The Faith of our Children,* notes, "The single most catalytic factor to influence the formation of lasting faith in children is loving, caring, adult relationships."[17] In Lifeway's book, *Flip the Script*, a heavy emphasis on relationships permeates, and the authors give an encouragement to lead with relationships before content: "Content that is conveyed in a context of trust and respect always yields greater influence."[18] Jesus provided the model for discipleship in his relationship with the disciples. Instead of discipling the masses or focusing his efforts on large crowds, Jesus chose to invest deeply and relationally with a small group of men who had little in common other than their calling to follow him.

While no one would dispute the effectiveness of Jesus's approach to discipleship, churches increasingly struggle to implement relational discipleship models. These four realities acknowledge the struggle churches face today:

---

[16] Brian Dembowczyk, *Family Discipleship That Works: Guiding Your Child to Know, Love, and Act Like Jesus* (IVP, 2024), 10.

[17] Matt Markins, *The Faith of Our Children: Eight Timely Research Insights for Discipling the Next Generation* (D6 Family Ministry, 2023), 19.

[18] Chuck Peters et al., *Flip the Script: Disrupting Tradition for the Sake of the Next Generation* (Lifeway Christian Resources, 2022), 66.

1. Children have a deficit of relationships in their lives. Concern for the mental health of children has never been higher, with loneliness and anxiety at all-time highs.[19]
2. Many Christian families no longer center their lives around participation in their faith community, making it difficult for relationships to flourish.
3. Sporadic church attendance and rotating volunteers in children's ministry make it difficult for children to experience belonging in their community of faith.
4. Ministry models have shifted to an overreliance on large-group approaches to accommodate the shortage of volunteers willing to consistently invest in the discipleship of children.

In many cases, children's ministers are caught between what works (pragmatism) and what is best for children. Without the participation and support of the entire faith community, these realities will continue to drive programming that may not be successful.

John Westerhoff, in his book, *Will Our Children Have Faith?*, emphasizes the need for children to be a part of an intergenerational faith community: "True community necessitates the presence and interaction of three generations."[20] Each generation has a significant role to play in the community. Some churches describe themselves as intergenerational, but the reality is that they are merely multigenerational. The presence and interaction Westerhoff described is

---

[19] "AAP-AACAP-CHA Declaration of a National Emergency in Child and Adolescent Mental Health," Aap.org, 2020, https://www.aap.org/en/advocacy/child-and-adolescent-healthy-mental-development/aap-aacap-cha-declaration-of-a-national-emergency-in-child-and-adolescent-mental-health/.

[20] John H. Westerhoff III, *Will Our Children Have Faith?*, 3rd rev. ed. (Morehouse, 2012), 53.

inhibited by the ministry models that separate generations based on worship styles. In effect, the younger generation worships in one room with their preferred style of music while the older generation meets in a different room designed to cater to their preferences. Generations rarely interact, and the benefit of intergenerational relationships is unrealized.

Bible Stories Are Foundational

Think for a moment about your favorite Bible story. Can you remember the first time you heard it? Why is it your favorite Bible story? Have you wondered about a missing detail or imagined what it might have been like to be an eyewitness to the story? "Stories are at the heart of faith development for children."[21] Jesus used parables (stories) to teach the disciples important truths he wanted them to understand. In the same way, children need to be taught important biblical concepts through engaging Bible stories.

Central to understanding the importance of story in child discipleship is the recognition of the Bible as the true story of God's work, culminating in the provision of Jesus to redeem and restore our relationship with him. Child discipleship does not exist without a reliance on God's Word to provide the foundation for all truth and spiritual formation. Consider these tips for embedding story into child discipleship:

1. Use curriculum that focuses on Bible stories rather than on topical issues or thematic approaches that overshadow biblical content. "Through the words of a masterful storyteller,

[21] Catherine Stonehouse, *Joining Children on the Spiritual Journey: Nurturing a Life of Faith* (Baker, 1998), 161.

we cross the Jordan River with the Israelites, we climb the tree with Zaccheus, and we stand at the foot of the cross with Jesus's disciples."[22]

2. Help children locate stories in their Bibles. Always have a physical Bible open as you tell the story.
3. Give children opportunities and space to respond to the story with curiosity and wonder.
4. Notice and normalize struggles, suffering, and mistakes made by people in Bible stories. Avoid the temptation to only emphasize the victories and miracles. Children need to know following Jesus is hard. Doubts and disillusionment can overwhelm their faith if there is not an expectation that living in a fallen world means they will experience times of suffering and distress. Otherwise, we may find "we have created a faith that is simplified. It's a faith that kids grow out of instead of a robust faith that they grow into."[23]

In addition to the powerful impact of well-told Bible stories, the community of faith needs to share their contemporary stories of God's faithfulness. In Deuteronomy 6, Moses delivers final instructions to the Israelites before they cross into the Promised Land. Within this chapter containing the greatest commandment and the Shema is an emphasis on telling the story of God's faithfulness to the next generation. The concern is that when the Israelites arrive in the Promised Land and begin to enjoy the benefits of living in a land

[22] Robert Keeley, *Helping Our Children Grow in Faith: How the Church Can Nurture the Spiritual Development of Kids* (Baker, 2008), 69.

[23] *Children's Ministry in a New Reality: Building Church Communities That Cultivate Lasting Faith* (Barna Group, 2022), 30.

flowing with milk and honey, they will forget it was the Lord who brought them out of Egypt. The Shema commands all of Israel to embed the story of God's deliverance into their everyday life through repetition and remembrance.

What does it look like for the community of faith to share their personal stories of God's faithfulness? Sometimes the most powerful stories are not spoken. Instead, they are lived out in ways that inspire, convict, and glorify the God who sustains and provides. Other times, stories are spoken through testimony or written down and shared with those who will read them. More importantly than how the stories are shared, children need to observe faithful, loving adults following Jesus through all of life's challenges and surprises, drawing attention not to themselves but to the God they serve. Do children in your faith community know the stories of God's faithfulness in the lives of the people in your faith community?

Rituals Foster Faith Formation

Children benefit from participation in the rituals of their faith communities because they provide an opportunity for children to express their faith in concrete and memorable ways. Children make meaning from what they participate in. A child learns to pray by praying. A child learns to worship by worshipping. In the OT, the people of God celebrated with feasts and festivals to reenact what God had done for them. In the NT, Jesus had the Last Supper with the disciples and utilized the symbolism of the bread and the cup to commemorate and embody what he was about to do for them through his death and resurrection. Consider these benefits for children as they participate in the rituals of their faith communities:

- Rituals serve as a conduit for children to experience connection, belonging, and meaning making.
- Rituals wire the brain for spiritual formation by creating and reinforcing the connections in the brain to foster faith formation.
- Rituals create a collective memory that can be accessed during times of difficulty and crisis. Synchronous, intergenerational rituals tie communities of faith together.
- Rituals "shape our understanding of who God is and what God values."[24]
- Rituals move children from spectators to full participants in their faith communities.

At least two venues in the local church provide an opportunity to include children in rituals. First, within the age-group structures, there are ministries specific to the child's age and development. Rituals in this space should be tailored to fit the developmental needs of the child. A consistent routine, a familiar greeting, a time of prayer, the use of repetition in the songs, and the intentional use of physical Bibles each week are rituals that help create a meaningful and predictable environment for children. One aspect of ritual often missing from the age-specific venue is the need for quiet reflection and reverence. Children can hear from God and respond to God when given the space to do so. There is a time for loud, fun, energetic songs, but there is also a need for children to slow down and think about how God may want them to respond.

The second venue for children's participation in rituals involves the church's corporate worship. Robbie Castleman reminds adults,

---

[24] Ivy Beckwith, *Formational Children's Ministry: Shaping Children Using Story, Ritual, and Relationship* (Baker, 2010), 72.

"Training children to worship is a zenith of sacred trust."[25] Careful consideration should be given to finding ways to bring the entire community of faith together to provide children an opportunity to participate as valuable and needed members of the faith community. Beyond welcoming and including children in worship, churches must find ways for them to be vitally involved. Invite children to read Scripture, voice a prayer, play an instrument, sing with the choir or praise team, or pass the offering plate. Children in corporate worship also observe two important ordinances of the church; baptism and the Lord's Supper. Involving children in meaningful ways in worship may be contradictory to recent worship trends of overvaluing production and polish and undervaluing the authenticity of imperfect worship and curious children. May we never grow tired of making room for the watching eyes and open hearts of children who need adults to teach them about the privilege of worship.

Doubts Must Be Addressed

Gaines Dobbins wrote,

> We who would conserve the fruit of evangelism must be alert to recognize the need of the child to express his doubts, to get his difficulties out in the open, and to be assured of sympathetic understanding as he struggles with conflicting ideologies.[26]

Doubts are often experienced by teenagers who made professions of faith as young children. It is common to hear a teenager say,

---

[25] Robbie F. Castleman, *Parenting in the Pew: Guiding Your Children in the Joy of Worship*, rev. ed. (IVP, 2013), 26.

[26] Dobbins, *Winning the Children*, 158.

"I am not sure I am really a Christian because I did not really understand what I was doing." How should the church respond to the doubts? There is no one response that can be used in every situation. However, there are a few principles to keep in mind:

1. Doubts are a signal that there is a need for dialogue. Ignoring doubts or immediately rushing a teenager to pray the prayer of salvation again are two common approaches that may not be helpful.
2. Doubts are an important part of the developmental tasks of faith formation. It is normal and expected for teenagers to question their childhood beliefs and come to a point of owning their beliefs. James Fowler, a faith development theorist, notes this in his description of a person moving from a "Synthetic-Conventional" stage of faith to an "Individuative-Reflective" stage of faith.[27]
3. Since doubts are often a normal part of the Christian experience, churches need to create an environment where tough questions are welcome and addressed without shame or condemnation.
4. Doubts can lead to a deeper faith. Consider the example of Thomas. Thomas was one of Jesus's disciples. He walked closely with Jesus, but he struggled to believe Jesus had risen without seeing with his own eyes the scars and putting his hands into the side of Jesus. Jesus answered the

[27] James Fowler, *Stages of Faith: The Psychology of Human Development and the Quest for Meaning* (Harper, 1981), 178–79. It is important to note that Fowler's concept of faith is different from historical Baptist definitions of a personal faith. His work is cited here to provide support for the developmental experiences of faith that often include working through doubts.

doubts of Thomas by drawing close to Thomas and allowing him to do the very thing he said he needed: "Then he said to Thomas, 'Put your finger here and look at my hands. Reach out your hand and put it into my side. Don't be faithless, but believe,'" (John 20:27). The response of Thomas was to acknowledge Jesus as "My Lord and my God!" (v. 28).

Recognition of these principles can help inform the ways in which teenagers are encouraged to work through doubts about their salvation. An adult-level understanding is not required for children to make a profession of faith. However, churches would do well to ensure individual counseling. A commitment to follow up with each child acknowledges and values the journey the child will be on and the developmental tasks of faith formation that extend well beyond childhood. More specifically, here are some tips that may preemptively help teenagers navigate the doubts about their salvation:

1. Anchor the memory of the event of salvation by writing down the details of the child's salvation experience so that the child can look back on a specific time and place when he or she made the decision to follow Jesus.
2. Involve parents in the process as much as possible. This means including parents in events where the gospel is being shared, training interested parents to lead their children to Christ, and providing materials for parents to disciple the child after salvation.
3. Make follow-up after the child's decision to follow Christ a high priority. New Christians classes often help children and their parents understand the importance of their decisions and the need for a lifetime of growth and discipleship.

4. Help children be assured of their salvation. There will be times when children and teenagers do not "feel" like followers of Christ. This is often due to sin or distancing from spiritual practices. Sometimes, the feelings of doubt or confusion are part of a recognition that there is a need to refocus or recenter one's life on Jesus.
5. Be open and supportive of the teenager who determines a true salvation experience did not occur in his or her childhood. After dialogue with the teenager about the doubts, recognize and respect the work of the Holy Spirit. Determining if a childhood salvation experience was real is not our job. Our responsibility and privilege is to walk alongside a teenager and make sure there is a space and time for him or her to have their questions explored and answered.

The task of discipling children utilizing the four areas of focus outlined in this chapter may seem overwhelming. One way to assess your ministry is to use the following tool to help you identify and evaluate areas of strength and weakness in your current practices. Take a few minutes and answer the following questions by placing a check in the box to the right of each statement that most closely identifies your ministry context.

	Yes	No
Relationships		
Children participate in church-wide events that provide opportunities for children to experience church as family.		
Children are taught by consistent adults who create environments where children are seen, heard, and valued.		

	Yes	No
Children are part of a small group where they can ask questions and engage relationally.		
Story		
The Bible is the focus of all learning and activities.		
Children are told Bible stories in ways that reflect a love for Scripture and an emphasis on the Bible as God's truth.		
Children hear stories from members of the community of faith that point them to a greater understanding of God's presence in their lives, even during difficult times.		
Children are given opportunities to tell their stories of God's faithfulness.		
Rituals		
Children are taught to pray, and prayer is a regular part of their experience at church.		
Children are given opportunities for both quiet reflection and energetic involvement.		
Children benefit from the routines and patterns intentionally established to create a safe and welcoming environment where faith formation can flourish.		
Children are given opportunities to be involved, and even lead, in corporate worship rituals.		
Doubts		
Doubts are embraced as opportunities for dialogue.		
Children know it is okay to ask questions about concepts they do not understand.		
Doubts are addressed with an understanding of the developmental tasks of faith formation.		

1. In which of the four areas of focus are you strongest? What convictions drive your ministry philosophy to value your area of strength?
2. In which of the four areas of focus are you weakest? What small step could you take to strengthen this area of focus?
3. If parents in your ministry filled out this assessment, what might be different about their view of your ministry?
4. How could you help parents understand the importance of each of these four areas of focus?

After reading this chapter and completing the assessment tool for best practices in child discipleship, what has God revealed to you about the state of child discipleship in your church? Discipling children is a long game with results that are hard to measure in real time. May we remember the words of Paul when he described young Timothy's faith: "And you know that from infancy you have known the sacred Scriptures, which are able to give you wisdom for salvation through faith in Christ Jesus" (2 Tim 3:15). There is an urgent need to better steward the time we have with children in the local church. God is still at work in the world and seeks a loving, lasting relationship with our children. The need for Christian adults in the church to commit to intentionally invest in the long game of faith formation in children has never been greater. The world will continue to win the battle for the hearts of our children unless we prioritize teaching children what it means to follow Christ and stand firm on the truths of the Bible.

Discussion Questions

1. This chapter encourages leaders to consider salvation as both an event and a process. Have you observed your

church leaning more toward a transaction-focused (event-focused) model or a transformation-focused (process-focused) model?
2. Name and discuss the four principles this chapter suggests to refocus efforts on the discipleship of children.
3. Have you observed "dechurching" at your church, as youth and young adults who grew up in church no longer choose to be involved? Why do you think this is a trend? What could we do in children's ministry to address this issue?
4. How can the church support parents in helping disciple children at home?

Opportunities for Application

- Complete the evaluation tool found in this chapter to help you discover specific areas to focus on relating to child discipleship.
- Evaluate your church's practices relative to the four areas:

    1. What does your church do well to help build relationships with children?
    2. How effectively does the curriculum you use address the need for Bible stories to be foundational?
    3. What rituals do children in your church participate in on a regular basis?
    4. Are children given opportunities to ask questions or dialogue about their doubts? How could you include more time for discussion in your current context of ministry?

- Consider the conversations you could have with parents, volunteers, and staff to address the importance of child discipleship.
- Find ways to celebrate both the event of salvation and the ongoing process of transformation.

CHAPTER 9

The Home and Spiritual Formation

Donna B. Peavey

The Goal of Parenting

"Then God said, 'Let us make man in our image, according to our likeness'" (Gen 1:26). The Bible declares that each child is made in the image of God, a designer original, personally formed by God.

> *For it was you who created my inward parts; you knit me together in my mother's womb. I will praise you, because I have been remarkably and wondrously made. Your works are wondrous, and I know this very well. My bones were not hidden from you when I was made in secret, when I was formed in the depths of the earth. (Ps 139:13–15)*

No child is an accident. While many children were not planned by their parents, they were planned by God. "God left no detail to chance. He planned it all for *his* purpose. . . . Nothing in your life is arbitrary. It's all for a purpose."[1] And what is that purpose? "You were made *by* God and *for* God—and until you understand that, life will never make sense."[2]

As with all people, each child "becomes accountable to his Creator for his words and actions. Each is dependent upon God for his fulfillment in life and his eternal destiny."[3] This is why teaching them from an early age to know, love, and obey God is important. While genes establish traits and some potential, a child's environment will have the greatest impact on who he or she becomes—and of all environments, the home has the most direct and significant impact on a child's development.

The home is the most significant environment, and parents are the greatest influence on their child—more than any other person in the world. They are responsible for protecting, teaching, encouraging, and meeting all the needs of their children—body, mind, spirit, and soul. These are challenging responsibilities, yet also the most rewarding. Parenting the whole child takes commitment.

Beyond meeting all of a child's needs, what is the end goal of parenting? Scripture indicates that parenting is about leading children to grow in their relationship with self, others, and God. Cos Davis asserts, "How we relate to self, others and God is what life is about."[4]

---

[1] Rick Warren, *The Purpose Driven Life: What on Earth Am I Here For?* (Zondervan, 2002), 23.

[2] Warren, 18.

[3] C. Sybil Waldrop, *Guiding Your Child Toward God* (Broadman, 1985), 14.

[4] Cos Davis, *Parenting with a Purpose: Biblical Foundations for Successful Parenting* (CrossBooks, 2009), 5.

Jesus spoke of the command to love self, others, and God when confronted by an expert in the law and challenged to identify the greatest of all commandments. Jesus's response was, "Love the Lord your God with all your heart, with all your soul, and with all your mind. This is the greatest and most important command. The second is like it: Love your neighbor as yourself. All the Law and the Prophets depend on these two commands" (Matt 22:37–40). The best time to model this commandment for children is when they are young.

Scripture says to "start a youth out on his way; even when he grows old he will not depart from it" (Prov 22:6). In *Revolutionary Parenting*, researcher George Barna stated that he discovered "what parents do with their youngsters prior to the teen years is of paramount importance to the Kingdom of God on earth."[5] Christian parents, the primary influencers on the faith of their children, must be intentional in discipling them in the home—the most consequential environment in which formation occurs.

Jesus's final command, to make disciples, is the central mission of all Christians, including parents (Matt 28:18–20). Making disciples is a proactive action—causing something to happen. God entrusts parents with the responsibility of discipling their children through teaching them his commands and through applying them to their daily lives. Many parents embrace this responsibility, striving to lead their children to love and serve God. However, not all Christian parents are obedient to the command. They may or may not attend church regularly, and their homes are often secular places where God is not central to family life. Regrettably, many children know only what they learn at church about God,

---

[5] George Barna, *Revolutionary Parenting: What the Research Shows Really Works* (Tyndale, 2007), xxi.

the Bible, prayer, and other religious things. This should not be. The foundation for faith must be built in the home, not the church only. In this chapter, we will examine the scriptural admonitions given to parents to teach their children. By doing such an examination, we can understand *why* the discipleship of children in the home is important.

Deuteronomy 6:4–9: The Shema—God's Command to Parents

Parents are commanded to pass their faith to their children. Deuteronomy 6:4–9, the Shema, is the clearest declaration of God's command to pass on his commands to children. This daily prayer of the ancient Israelites gets its name from the first Hebrew word of the passage, *shema*, which can be translated "hear" or "listen." Eugene Merrill states, "'To hear,' in the Hebrew lexicography, is tantamount to 'to obey,' especially in covenant contexts such as this. That is, to hear God without putting into effect the command is not to hear him at all."[6] Jesus gave weight to the Shema—referring to it several times (Mark 12:30, Luke 10:27; 11:42).

> "Listen, Israel: The LORD our God, the LORD is one. Love the LORD your God with all your heart, with all your soul, and with all your strength. These words that I am giving you today are to be in your heart. Repeat them to your children. Talk about them when you sit in your house and when you walk along the road, when you lie down and when you get up. Bind them as a sign on your hand and let them be a

[6] Eugene H. Merrill, *Deuteronomy*, NAC 4 (B&H, 1994), 162.

symbol on your forehead. Write them on the doorposts of your house and on your city gates." (Deut 6:4–9)

Moses began by addressing a wide audience—a new generation of Israel—as they were preparing to enter the Promised Land. He told *all* of Israel, the entire covenant community, to listen to God and love him above everything else, as their obedience to God would influence the direction of their people when they enter the Promised Land. Moses then focused on parents and the faith formation of their children, in order that they might experience the full blessing of the Promised Land. The parents' obedience would lead to blessings.

The Israelite parents were *first* to internalize the commandments and *then* teach their children. God's instructions through Moses were quite specific. He was clear as to where, when, and how they were to teach their children.

Israelite parents were instructed to use repetition as a means of teaching their children. To keep the Word of God constantly before the family, they were instructed to post it on the doorframe of the house, where they would see it each time they entered and left the home. Daniel Block stated, "This covenant commitment is to be a family matter, demonstrated by the indoctrination of children and the spontaneous discussion of the issue with the members of one's household."[7] He further stated that the purpose of the elements in the Shema was to mark the Israelites as people who claimed Yahweh as their covenant Lord and who were committed to loving him. The Shema provided the Israelites with a constant

[7] Daniel Block, *Deuteronomy*, NIV Application Commentary (Zondervan, 2012), 184.

reminder to commit themselves to Yahweh alone.[8] In *Studies in Deuteronomy,* Donald Ackland describes three kinds of love of man for God.

1. Obedient love—"God has made known his will for his people. For them, therefore, the highest expression of love is obedience to his revealed will."
2. Undivided love—This is the love of the total person.
3. Reverential love—"Under love's constraint, response to God's laws becomes a matter of willing, happy acquiescence."[9]

This love was to be translated into practice. The people's obedience acknowledged their indebtedness to God and demonstrated their loyalty to him. While the law was given to Israel, the faith was personal—to be taught to their children.

Application of the Shema to Contemporary Families

Mark Biddle asserts, "The Shema calls believers to re-center their lives in relationship to the one God of Israel, the father of Jesus Christ"[10] and presents the following assertions that speak to contemporary life:

1. The Lord is one. This declaration reminds those who confess the Shema that God can be trusted to remain constant to his purposes.

---

[8] Block, 186–88.

[9] Donald Ackland, *Studies in Deuteronomy* (Convention Press, 1964), 56–57.

[10] Mark Biddle, *Deuteronomy*, Smyth & Helwys Bible Commentary (Smyth & Helwys, 2003), 131.

2. Shema calls for unsentimental obedience to the claims of the one Lord on believers' lives. He will not be satisfied to be the object of warm feelings.
3. Shema addresses the character of the life devoted to God. Obedience of God's people must be total.[11]

How are these three declarations manifested in the contemporary family? First, *God is constant to his purposes*—the same yesterday, today, and forever. The law of Moses was fulfilled in Christ (Matt 5:17). Today, Christians are called to obey the "law of Christ," a law of love (John 13:34–35). Referring to the OT, Jesus said, "Love the Lord your God with all your heart, with all your soul, and with all your mind. This is the greatest and most important command. The second is like it: Love your neighbor as yourself. All the Law and the Prophets depend on these two commands" (Matt 22:37–40). The end goal of parenting—that the children will grow to love God with all of their hearts, souls, and minds—is the same today as yesterday.

Second, *God requires loving obedience. Parents who are passionate about God will live this out in the family, overflowing onto their children.* Christians are required to demonstrate obedience to God out of love for him (John 14:23). God does not want his children merely to think of him fondly but to be passionate about him, not lukewarm. In Isa 29:13–14, God addresses this. "The Lord said: These people approach me with their speeches to honor me with lip-service, yet their hearts are far from me, and human rules direct their worship of me. Therefore, I will again confound these people with wonder after wonder." In a NT letter to the church at Laodicea, Jesus says, "I know your works, that you are neither cold nor hot. I wish that you were

---

[11] Biddle, 131–32.

cold or hot. So, because you are lukewarm, and neither hot nor cold, I am going to vomit you out of my mouth" (Rev 3:15–16).

Parents have a responsibility to lead their children to passionately love God and his Word. As a children's Sunday school teacher, in order to develop a love for reading God's Word at home and church, I partner with parents in encouraging their children to read their Bibles through the week and bring them to Bible study. A daughter of *active members* brought her Bible each week. When I expressed to her mother how glad I was that she did so, her mom responded excitedly, "She will have it every Sunday—we leave it in the trunk of the car!" What a message this sent to her daughter—that her Bible was for Sunday use only—a lukewarm practice. Another child, when offered a prize for reading her Bible daily through the week said, "I like reading the Bible every day. I don't need the prize." She had developed a passion for God's Word—supported by her parents and her church.

Third, *today's parents are instructed to live the truth—unconsciously teaching who they are in front of their children.* Their love of God should be on full display. As with the Israelites, character matters. Parents can only teach what they have internalized. To raise children with a living faith, parents must be immersed in it themselves.

The Shema highlights the importance of informal teaching—those things that parents do every day. For children, this is learning "on the go," not just during formal teaching times. Clearly, the instruction is meant to cover all aspects of daily life. Parents must take advantage of each opportunity to communicate spiritual truths. Family conversations about God should be as natural as other conversations. Parents can leverage instances of sitting at home, walking along the road, lying down, and getting up by uttering a blessing before eating, going for a walk and thanking God for the evening breeze, or saying evening prayers. Block purports that "this passage suggests that the very decoration of our homes should bear testimony to our faith, declaring to all guests and passers-by the fundamentally theological outlook of those who live within, and serving as reminders to residents to live in dependence on God and to realize that blessing is contingent on obedience."[12]

The Practice of Spiritual Disciplines

Donald Whitney defines spiritual disciplines as "those personal and corporate disciplines that promote spiritual growth."[13] The best context for such practice is the home. Consistently living the truth in front of children leads them to develop relationships with God, self, and others. When exercised regularly, spiritual disciplines and practices of the Christian faith support faith development.

Disciplines include practices such as meditation, prayer, study, service, and worship. The spiritual disciplines should be practiced often, because children learn through experience and the repetition of practices that are associated with what is important. For example, praying together each day helps a child identify the practice as significant. For parents, modeling the commitment to practice spiritual disciplines is a sacred responsibility. A brief description of several spiritual disciplines in which children can engage follows. This is not an exhaustive list. (Children respond to the word "practice" better than they do to the word "discipline.") A number of resources are

---

[12] Block, *Deuteronomy*, 189.

[13] Donald Whitney, *Spiritual Disciplines for the Christian Life* (NavPress, 1991), 17.

available for parents that include age-appropriate suggestions for the practice of the disciplines.

Meditation

The Cambridge Dictionary defines "ponder" as "to think carefully about something, especially for a noticeable length of time."[14] Children should spend time *pondering*—asking questions, meditating on answers, and asking more questions. They are designed by God to ask questions, and they need to be able to rely on the most significant adults in their lives, parents, to respond. Meditation helps children to know, understand, and internalize God's Word and biblical truths and leads to the formation of godly character.

Prayer

Prayer, talking to God, is the first spiritual discipline most Christian parents teach their children. Even very young children can pray. Parents should give children opportunities to pray for themselves and others. Modeling prayer for children provides a language for prayer that makes it familiar.

Bible Study

Bible study is setting aside time to study God's Word for the purpose of understanding. The best way for children to study the Bible and learn biblical truths is to read the Bible and talk about it with

[14] https://dictionary.cambridge.org/us/dictionary/english/ponder.

adults they trust. Providing a children's Bible and other study tools will encourage them to read God's Word.

Service

Service is helping others. When parents lead children to serve others, the greatest commandments—to love God and love your neighbor—are put into practice. Parents should serve alongside their children and express joy in the service, reminding them that service gives them the opportunity to be found "good and faithful" (Matt 25:21).

Family Worship

Family worship is a time for the family to read God's Word, pray, and sing hymns or praise songs. Children of all ages can participate. To make family worship a priority, parents may need to adjust the family's busy schedule. Unless it is intentionally scheduled, it is likely to get superseded by other activities.

Does the practice of the spiritual disciplines pay off? Lifeway Research investigated what parenting practices experienced by children resulted in higher spiritual health when they became young adults. They found that the *behavior of parents* is related to their young adult children's spiritual health. The researchers found that young adults had higher spiritual health scores if their parents had spent time during their childhood doing the following:

- "Reading the Bible several times a week."
- "Taking part in a service project or church mission trip as a family."
- "Sharing their faith with unbelievers."

- "Encouraging teenagers to serve in church."

Lifeway Research found that Bible reading as a child was the top factor in determining the spiritual health of the young adults they surveyed.[15] They also found that participating in Bible reading, prayer, service, listening to Christian music, and mission trips in childhood could raise a young adult's spiritual health score by 41 percent and put them above the 90th percentile.[16]

Other Influences on Spiritual Formation

Research indicates that even in the early stages of development, children are capable of spiritual experiences.[17] The spiritual understanding a child develops in the first twelve years usually forms the basis for beliefs in adulthood. Barna stated, "Thanks to my research related to child development and spiritual growth, I have become convinced that the spiritual war occurring in individual lives is pretty much won or lost by the age of thirteen."[18] The first six years of life are especially critical in laying the foundation that must support a lifetime of experiences.

Developmental theories recognize the impact of family relationships and experiences on a child's development, and they recognize that the relationship between parent and child is perhaps the most

---

[15] Lifeway Research, "Young Bible Readers More Likely to be Faithful Adults, Study Finds," Lifeway Christian Resources, October 17, 2017, https://research.lifeway.com/2017/10/17/young-bible-readers-more-likely-to-be-faithful-adults-study-finds/.

[16] Lifeway Research.

[17] Ronald Goldman, *Religious Thinking from Childhood to Adolescence* (Routledge & Kegan Paul, 1964).

[18] Barna, *Revolutionary Parenting*, xxi.

influential one.[19] From their earliest days, children learn by imitating parents and participating in the family. Babies can learn about God through their senses before they learn through *words.* Before they understand words, babies can interpret tone of voice, facial expressions, and touch. They live in a state of sensory learning. In this stage, faith foundations are sensed and nurtured through relationships, primarily in the home. The role of the parent "is to demonstrate love to your child even before he can begin to understand that God exists or that God loves him. You are the first human bridge to your child's acceptance of the fact that God loves him."[20]

Our daughter was born on a Saturday morning. When I awoke on Sunday, my husband was cradling her in his arms and reading to her out of a children's Bible gifted to her upon her birth. She was being held lovingly, being spoken to in a soft and gentle tone, hearing the Word of God, and experiencing what I call a *sensory bath.* While she *did not understand* the words, she *could sense* a loving and trusting environment drawn from her dad's love and devotion to God. Her earthly father was already preparing her for a relationship with her Creator.

Babies enter the world with the senses to experience God's creation, including human relationships. Before they are verbal, babies engage in relationships with significant people—mother, father, grandparents, and siblings, for example—through which they learn valuable things that become part of the foundation for their lives. For example, when parents consistently respond to their baby's cry, the baby learns that the parents can be trusted; this is unconscious learning—learning without words. "The teaching without words

---

[19] Erik Erikson, "Eight Ages of Man," in *Childhood and Society* (W. W. Norton, 1985); Bowlby, John, *Attachment*, vol. 1, *Attachment and Loss* (Basic Books, 1969).

[20] Davis, *Parenting with Purpose*, 7.

must precede the use of words, or the words will never be fully understood. The life before words are understood begins in the home in the life of the little child. Before he can understand words he learns many important things that help build the foundation of his life."[21]

Erik Erikson, a leading psychologist of the twentieth century, proposed that basic trust is an attitude derived from the experiences of the first year of life and that a parent's faith is transmitted to his child in the form of basic trust.[22] *A child must develop a sense of trust to establish healthy relationships with others and God.* A child will have a difficult time understanding God as loving if his first experiences in life do not lead to the establishment of trust and healthy attachment.

For a child to know and love God is the goal, and a child's faith flows from his God concepts. In *The Children's God*, David Heller identified three influences on a child's developing God concept: communication with parents and other members of the family about religious concepts and rituals, the child's interpretation of the family atmosphere and parents, and the child's self-concept.[23] Other research finds much the same—that the factors influencing God concepts include parent religiosity, religious training in the family, and the family's denomination. Of all factors, parents are the most important influence in a child's development of God concepts.[24] When parents spend time talking about a subject with their children, it indicates that it is valuable to them. When they talk about

---

[21] Anna Mow, *Your Child from Birth to Rebirth: How to Educate Your Child to Be Ready for a Life with God* (Zondervan, 1972), 26.

[22] Erikson, "Eight Ages of Man."

[23] David Heller, *The Children's God* (University of Chicago Press, 1986), 108.

[24] Lifeway Research, "Young Bible Readers."

the Bible, God, Jesus, their faith, or the church, that sends a message to the child that it is important.

All children need correction, and the style of discipline a parent employs influences a child's developing God concept. When parents view God as loving, there is a greater tendency for their children to view them as loving.[25] When loving parents discipline their children with love-oriented discipline, the result is concepts of a nurturing and powerful God.[26] However, the more parents use strict, power-assertive techniques, the more their children view God as angry.[27] When the occasion merits it, parents can model for children how God lovingly corrects and forgives. Correction should be restorative, not just punitive. As the Shema instructs, repetition is key. A child will understand forgiveness when he or she consistently and lovingly experiences it. When our daughter was young, she occasionally had to "sit" because of unacceptable behavior. When she expressed remorse for what she had done and asked for forgiveness, I always told her she was forgiven, hugged her, and then wiped my forehead saying, "I don't even remember what you did. We have a do-over." In this manner, I modeled how God always forgives when we ask for it, and he chooses to remember our sins no more.

Parents need to make regular attendance at church a priority, as it has an impact on a child's God concepts. Research shows that children who attend church regularly have a more positive God concept

---

[25] Bradley R. Hertel and Michael J. Donahue, "Parental Influences on God Images among Children: Testing Durkheim's Metaphoric Parallelism," *JSSR* 34, no. 2 (1995): 186–99.

[26] Jane R. Dickie et al., "Parent-Child Relationships and Children's Images of God," *JSSR* 36, no. 1 (1997): 25–43.

[27] Simone A. de Roos et al., "Influence of Maternal Denomination, God Concepts, and Child-Rearing Practices on Young Children's God Concepts," *JSSR* 43, no. 4 (2004): 519–35.

than those who attend occasionally.[28] The more children are exposed to God through Bible study and worship, the greater their understanding and love for him will be.

Through the Bible, God provides instructions for relationships with others and him. Following these instructions, parents should engage children in a loving relationship, rooted in their love for God. Through a healthy parent-child relationship, they should guide their child to experience God and love him. Research by man supports what God has instructed. As was true for the Israelite parents, obedience from love of God by contemporary parents and children will lead to blessings. The following conclusions may be drawn from the biblical text and man's research:

1. Parents are the most significant influence on their children.
2. The family is the primary context for the development of faith.
3. The way parents model their faith in daily life influences the faith development of their children and the development of God-concepts.
4. The quality of the parent-child relationship, parenting style, and discipline techniques greatly influence faith development.

Discussion Questions

1. What is the goal of Christian parenting?
2. God instructed his people to love him with all their hearts, souls, and minds. How can the church guide parents to obey God's instruction in the Shema?

---

[28] Mariana Hwang, "Understanding Korean-American Children's God-Concept in Relation to Their Self-Concept Development," *Christian Education Journal* 2, no. 2 (2005): 282–301.

3. How can the local church equip and encourage parents to practice spiritual disciplines with their children?
4. What measures can the local church take to enhance family communication and the overall health of families to facilitate the development of positive God-concepts?

Opportunities for Application

- Consider your church's parent ministry and how it can intentionally equip parents for the role of spiritual leader in the home. Workshops and seminars for parents could address topics such as age-appropriate discipline techniques, spiritual disciplines, and communication, among others.
- As presented in the chapter, numerous factors influence the development of God-concepts and faith. Considering this, determine what your church is doing to influence preschoolers and children as they develop faith and concepts of God.
- Parents are often willing to engage in spiritual disciplines with their children but feel ill-equipped to do so. Consider ways in which parents of preschoolers and children may be equipped, such as mentoring by an older parent, seminars, workshops, or available literature. Prepare a parent library that includes books, brochures, and videos.
- Examine your church's calendar and publications. In what ways do they reflect the church's commitment to support parents in raising children to know and passionately love God?

CHAPTER 10

Evangelizing Children and Catechesis

W. Madison Grace II

There is nothing more pressing for Christian parents than the eternal condition of our children. We want to see them come to the same place of faith that we have received from the Lord. The difficulty is that our children are autonomous selves and cursed by sin the same way that we all are. We cannot make them have faith any more than someone can make us have faith. The parental desire is strong for our children to make a decision for Christ, and parents are central to that process. There is action we must take, but we want to ensure that we are engaging them and leading them in the right manner. Simply having a nominal confession is not enough, for that saves no one. Too many have depended on an external action, like walking an aisle, repeating a prayer, or even going through with baptism. Without true conversion, these actions are nothing more than lip service deceiving a child into a false hope. True, authentic faith is that which evidences regeneration in our children's lives. Our dependence is on the divine intervention that comes by the Holy Spirit, and we have very little control (if any) over that transforming power.

Does this mean we are powerless? If not, is there anything that we can do to assist in this process? Of course there is, and it is part of the biblical mandate of parenting. Building on Prov 22:6—"Start a youth out on his way; even when he grows old he will not depart from it"—we have the warrant and necessity to be actively involved in the development of the lives of our children. Other translations use the phrase "train up," indicating a call for direct action from the parent. We are to train our children in the ways of the world. We do this in many ways—jobs and chores, etiquette and manners, etc.—but it is of greater importance that we are training them up in the way of faith, holiness, and godliness.

It is imperative that parents are the ones doing this training. There is a necessary partnership with the community of the local church, who should come alongside and assist in this task. Thank goodness God has not called us to do this completely alone, but that does not change the fact that it is the parents' responsibility to train their own children. Through this chapter we will look more closely at ways that we can engage in that training called *catechesis*. This looks like a million-dollar word that may be too complex to understand, but it is not. *Catechesis* is just an old word transliterated from another language that helps describe a simple task of teaching children the key aspects of the Christian faith and doctrine.

The aim of this chapter is to look closely at the task of training up a child by means of catechesis and the formal tool called a catechism. To do so, I will set the stage for the need of catechesis with a reminder of the humanity that all children possess. Then, we will turn to defining catechesis and catechisms clearly. Finally, we will look at practical engagement in this process with children and provide some simple ways that any parent can begin this process.

Basic Anthropology

I believe it is important that we take a moment to reflect on what a child is before engaging in processes and tools for training children. They are not simply machines that must be programmed, nor are they animals that merely respond to certain criteria. We need to know what we are called to train, and that *what* is a *person* created in the *image of God.*

When we use the term "person," we might not understand or articulate all of what needs to be assumed in the concept. When some think of a person walking down the street, they may simply think of another body that is coming their way. The person is a unit of matter that is taking up space and energy in a particular way—in this case, observed on any given street. This type of thinking is not wrong, but it is incomplete at best and is a reduction of personal identity to material substances. It can lead to an understanding of a person as nothing more than mere material existing in our world that is not greater or lesser than any number of other pieces of matter that could also assume that same space in time—say a dog, tree, or boulder. It should not take long to recognize this is not what most mean, especially Christians, when we use the term "person."

So, what do we mean when we say we are more than mere material and valued as such? The sixth-century Christian philosopher Boethius famously defined a person as "the individual substance of a rational nature."[1] Surely this definition gets us closer than the reductionistic concept of persons above, but it still is a bit opaque. Acknowledging the rational state of a human person sets the human person apart from other parts of the created order (even though we can see advanced cognition in a variety of animals); however, it raises other questions about what humanity is. As human nature was considered and differentiated from other parts of creation, it became common to distinguish between what a human, or a person, *is* and what one *does*. There is a distinction to a person that exists apart from what he or she does, what Robert Spaemann discusses as *nature*. "[Human beings'] nature is not what they *are*, pure and simple; their nature is something that they *have*. And this 'having' is their being. To be a person is the form in which 'rational natures' exist."[2] Spaemann continues his discussion by pointing out that there are other natures existent in the natural order. We can see animals existing with these natures that predetermine how they act—which is according to their nature. But this concept of nature means something different when we think of human nature. He concludes his discussion,

> With the concept of the person, however, we come to think of the particular individual as being more basic than its nature. This is not to suggest that these individuals *have* no nature, and start out by deciding for themselves what they are to be. What they do is assume a new relation to their nature; they freely endorse the laws of their being, or alternatively they

[1] Boethius, *Contra Eutychen et Nestorium*, trans. H. F. Stewart et al., Loeb Classical Library 74 (Harvard University Press, 1973), 85.

[2] Robert Spaemann, *Persons: The Difference Between Someone and Something*, trans. Oliver O'Donovan, Oxford Studies in Theological Ethics (Oxford University Press, 2006), 31.

> rebel against them and 'deviate.' Because they are thinking beings, they cannot be categorized exhaustively as members of their species, only as individuals, who 'exist *in* their nature.' That is to say, they exist as persons.[3]

What Spaemann is intimating is that we need to consider all humans in their individual natures as those that are free to act on their nature in individual ways that are not reduced to broad categories. Though there are common ways of being a person, human personhood points to our individuality, and that individuality, autonomous as it is, separates us from every other human. That particularity is something bequeathed to us at birth and not something that we grow into or determine for ourselves, a point that is of importance when we contemplate children as persons. They are individuals created with form and purpose by their Creator.

Biblically, the form and purpose of humanity was set from the beginning of creation. When God created humans, he did so in a particular way that sets us all apart from the rest of creation. We see this most clearly in Gen 1:26–27:

> Then God said, 'Let us make man in our image, according to our likeness. They will rule the fish of the sea, the birds of the sky, the livestock, the whole earth, and the creatures that crawl on the earth.' So God created man in his own image; he created him in the image of God; he created them male and female.

This passage is foundational for thinking about what a human is. We must begin here lest we run afoul and think that our created

---

[3] Spaemann, 33.

selves are somewhat the same as birds, or something of that sort. What is of greatest importance in this text is realizing that every human—male and female—is created in the *image* and *likeness* of God. This is language unique to humans and not found in reference to any other part of creation, no matter how much we think we can see cognitive similarities. Humans are unique. Consider Ps 139:14, "I will praise you because I have been remarkably and wondrously made." These statements about humanity point to the image in which humans are created—an image that is of God himself. There are pages upon pages written about what being created in this image means, and although helpful, they generally all fall into three different categories or models: substantive, functional, or relational.[4] Wherever one lands on this question, I think it is important to note that humans are different from the rest of creation in the sense that we have the ability to engage God in ways other created beings cannot. We have the capacity to know God, and that *knowing* is founded in our nature.

These concepts—personhood and image—are helpful for looking at any human and seeing in him or her an individual nature, with its autonomy, that has the capacity to relate with its Creator. This capacity is predicated on the whole person that is in the image, which is both spirit *and* body. We are not mere spirits finding our way to God but embodied persons living life in this world for God until he takes us home. This capacity is natural from one's beginning in such a way that our God can relate to us but also holds us accountable to the obedience that he has demanded

[4] For more information see John S. Hammett and Katie J. McCoy, "Created in the Image of God," chap. 3 in *Humanity*, Theology for the People of God, ed. David S. Dockery et al. (B&H Academic, 2023).

of humans since the creation of Adam. Romans 5 addresses this concern clearly:

> Therefore, just as sin entered the world through one man, and death through sin, in this way death spread to all people, because all sinned. In fact, sin was in the world before the law, but sin is not charged to a person's account when there is no law. Nevertheless, death reigned from Adam to Moses, even over those who did not sin in the likeness of Adam's transgression. He is a type of the Coming One. . . .
>
> So then, as through one trespass there is condemnation for everyone, so also through one righteous act there is justification leading to life for everyone. For just as through one man's disobedience the many were made sinners, so also through the one man's obedience the many will be made righteous. The law came along to multiply the trespass. But where sin multiplied, grace multiplied even more so that, just as sin reigned in death, so also grace will reign through righteousness, resulting in eternal life through Jesus Christ our Lord. (vv. 12–14, 18–21)

Here we see the reality of our human condition in the present state. We are created in the image of God. We have seen that humans in their individuated state were free to obey or disobey, and they chose disobedience. As a result, sin and condemnation came to all of Adam's progeny (who are not in any better state to make better choices than Adam). But we also see that the salvation that comes to humanity comes in the form of a man who could be like us in every way excepting sin—able to be the righteousness that overcomes our disobedience. This eternal exchange is only possible for those created in such a way that they can know God and, further, can be with

God as those who can cry out "Abba, Father." Our unique anthropology as humans—persons created in the image of God—allows us the ability to relate to God, but we must do so as individuals who seek God while he may be found. Having a capacity to know God does not mean anyone is guaranteed to know him. We all need to be instructed and taught as we instruct and teach others.

Training by Catechesis

The author of Hebrews takes a moment in the middle of his discourse to comment on the state of his readers, "Although by this time you ought to be teachers, you need someone to teach you the basic principles of God's revelation again. You need milk, not solid food" (Heb 5:12). This statement is intended to help us see the need to grow in our knowledge of the truth, yet many remain unlearned, as infants who are on milk and lack the maturity to eat solid food. The timeless truth here we need to note is that training or teaching is necessary for the Christian life. The people of God throughout the Bible have always been in need of someone to instruct them. Whether it was the law, a prophet, or a rabbi like Jesus, humans need to have instruction. Our nature does not come preloaded with the intuition to live a godly life and seek God. We must be taught. This can come in a variety of forms, including preaching and teaching, but it also comes in the form of a process called *catechesis*.

Catechesis is a word derived from the Greek word, *katēcheō*, which simply means "to teach" or "to instruct." Though in what follows we will discuss more formalized forms of catechesis, especially as it develops into various forms of catechisms, the basic idea of catechesis is bound up in teaching or instructing. Consider these passages that use this word:

Luke 1:4—"So that you may know the certainty of the things about which you have been *instructed*."

Acts 18:25—"He had been *instructed* in the way of the Lord;"
Gal 6:6—"Let the one who is *taught* the word share all his good things with the teacher."[5]

Each of these texts sits in its own context, yet all point to the way in which instruction and teaching was part of the life of the early church. As we think about evangelizing children, we need to remember to what we are calling them. It is to a *real* faith with corresponding *real* doctrines and teachings. These doctrines are the basis of the gospel. The good news of Jesus Christ is predicated on significant dogmatic truths, deviation from which can lead to dire consequences. Teaching is part and parcel to transmitting the gospel because the gospel is full of theological content. This is why Paul, in Rom 10:14–15, asks,

> How, then, can they call on him they have not believed in? And how can they believe without hearing about him? And how can they hear without a preacher? And how can they preach unless they are sent? As it is written: How beautiful are the feet of those who bring good news.

As we can see, the process of salvation includes the preaching task, which inevitably requires teachable content to be transmitted. Sure, this is a work of God, and we are dependent on the Holy Spirit's engagement with hearts, but it happens alongside the teaching and preaching of the Word of God. Catechesis is simply the task of Christians to train and instruct the lost, the immature, or even the seasoned Christian. It can be formal or informal, but it is a

---

[5] Emphasis added.

necessary part of making disciples as seen in the Great Commission in Matt 28:19–20, "Go, therefore, and make disciples of all nations, baptizing them in the name of the Father and of the Son and of the Holy Spirit, teaching them to observe everything I have commanded you. And remember, I am with you always, to the end of the age." Part of making disciples is teaching the truths of God. Those who are interested in making disciples are those who are also interested in catechesis.

As Christianity grew from the first century into post-apostolic times, the process of catechesis took on a more formal setting. Catechetical work is found in the early church in the way they prepared converts for baptism. Before the advent of infant baptism, the initiatory rite of baptism was often performed on converts only after they had been instructed in the doctrines of the faith. These candidates for baptism were called *catechumens*, and this practice demonstrates the pre-baptismal instruction of the early church. Many church fathers wrote manuals on how to instruct the catechumens, to assist in this important process before allowing the catechumens to become part of the church and its practices.

As time marched forward, formal manuals were written to help teach and explain the Bible, especially the Decalogue, the Apostles' Creed, and the Lord's Prayer. By the time of the Reformation, this process was codified in what is more commonly known as a *catechism*. Simply defined, catechisms are "popular manuals of instruction . . . in Christian beliefs, normally in question-and-answer form. The word was not used in this sense until the early sixteenth century."[6] Children were often the main pupils of the catechisms, and

[6] D. F. Wright, "Catechisms," in *Evangelical Dictionary of Theology*, 3rd ed., ed. Daniel J. Treier and Walter A. Elwell (Baker Academic, 2017), 160.

completion of the material was the basis for confirmation, at which time the child is able to participate fully with the church in his or her first communion. In Baptist churches, who did not practice infant baptism, the practice of catechesis was just as popular and was used as a tool to teach children the truths of the Bible and to help them understand the gospel and basic doctrine.

In summary, catechesis is a particular way to understand instruction and teaching, especially for converts and future converts. The more formal process of a catechism is a tool that can be greatly helpful in ensuring that right belief is passed down and the purity of truth is transmitted so individuals can come to know God and grow in him.

Methods

Children in their created state have the capacity to know the things of God as much as they have the capacity to rebel against him. A directed process of teaching and instruction is not just beneficial but necessary for children if they are going to come to know God and follow him. But what does it really look like? I would like to conclude this chapter with a look at both formal and informal ways to engage catechesis with children, with the hope that it becomes a stronger and more prevalent practice and tool for Christian parents and churches.

Formal Means

The most formal way to engage in catechesis is to utilize a guide like a catechism. Some of the most famous catechisms are the Geneva Catechism, the Westminster Catechisms, and the Heidelberg Catechism. A popular adaptation of all three of these is found today in the *New City Catechism*. Baptists have historically used catechisms such as *Keach's Catechism* or *A Catechism of Bible Teaching* by John Broadus as well.[7] The basic format is a question and an answer that are intended to be memorized and discussed. For example, here are the first two questions from *Keach's Catechism*:

Q. 1. *Who is the first and best of beings?*
A. God is the first and best of beings.
Q. 2. *Ought every one to believe there is a God?*
A. Every one ought to believe there is a God, and it is their great sin and folly who do not.[8]

Notice in these two questions the depth of thought formed in simple language. When any person, and children most of all, begin to imagine what is out there, simple guidance is all that is needed. Catechistic questions allow for this directed guidance, and these questions put up the guardrails of thought about what is foundational to faith and the truth of God revealed in Scripture. For instance, when a child is having anxiety about what happens to them at death, a parent can easily set the parameters of the discussion. Consider these questions from Broadus's catechism:

Q. What becomes of the soul at death?
A. The soul is undying, and passes at once into blessedness or suffering. (2 Cor 5:8; Luke 16:23, 28)
Q. What becomes of the body after death?

---

[7] See Tom J. Nettles, *Teaching Truth, Training Hearts: The Study of Catechisms in Baptist Life* (Calvary, 1998).

[8] Benjamin Keach, *The Baptist Catechism, Commonly Called Keach's Catechism: Or, a Brief Instruction in the Principles of the Christian Religion* (American Baptist Publication Society, 1851), 3.

A. The body returns to dust, but it will rise again. (Gen 3:19; Eccl 12:7; Acts 24:15)[9]

Though these two questions may elicit many more questions from all of us, especially children, they provide the foundational doctrinal truth from Scripture that provides a way forward in understanding the eternal truths and mysteries of God.

These catechisms can be utilized in many different places. They can be part of a family gathering or instituted into a small-group curriculum. They can be a part of training parents for discipling their own children or training for children's leaders in the church. This also can be something formally utilized for the whole church and become part of the church's worship practice, wherein a question is read and answered every week. In this way, the catechism functions much the same way as does a memory verse. The aim is the same, teaching truth to form minds—or catechesis.

Informal Means

For some, the above practices may seem too intimidating for their church. This does not mean that one cannot engage in catechesis. It is still the imperative for the parent to train up the child in the way he or she will go. There needs to be spiritual and theological training, however foundational, and that training needs to have some intentionality behind it, or it will never happen. This is where catechesis is of great help, and it can be very simple.

The easiest way to ensure that evangelism and instruction are occurring is to engage in regular *conversations* with children. In a world where

---

[9] Nettles, *Teaching Truth, Training Hearts*, 218.

we all are distracted by digital devices, parents often lose the ability to have regular conversations with their children. When conversations do occur, are children met where they are with their many questions about life, the world around them, and that which is beyond? Here the opportunity to converse about theological truth leads to informal avenues of catechizing children with the main tenets of the faith, leading to salvation and into discipleship. Conversations with our children about God, the gospel, right and wrong, and holiness need to begin from the earliest possible moments. These conversations are not as hard to have as they may seem, but they must be intentional. Whether you have a regular dinner scheduled or are optimizing carpool time, these conversations can change the trajectory of a child for life.

Finally, this task may seem to be too much to handle for some due to the inadequacies a parent may feel. Parents may think, "We do not know the Bible as well as we would like. We do not know how to share our faith, so how can we share with our children? We do not model the holiness that we know our children need to see. So how can we be the ones to evangelize and catechize our children?" No one has perfect knowledge, but all have some knowledge. Share what you know.

Conclusion

The task of evangelizing and teaching truth to children is not one that should be overcomplicated. Children are created exactly the same as adults but need shaping and forming. It is the parents' responsibility to train their children so that when they grow old, they will not depart from the way that brings life. In this chapter, we investigated the anthropological nature of humanity and showed that all, including children, have the capacity to know God since they are individual persons created in God's image. Yet it is the responsibility of

Christian parents and churches to engage and facilitate the task of training these children in the teachings of God. Whether it be formal catechisms or informal theological conversations, children need to be taught so they can glorify God and enjoy him forever.

Discussion Questions

1. In what ways could using a formal catechism be helpful for yourself or others?
2. What are some catechetical conversations that have been helpful?
3. How can catechesis become more prominent in your children's ministry?
4. What are some ways to engage in catechesis with children whose parents are not Christians or engaged in church?

Opportunities for Application

- Reviewing the catechisms noted in this chapter, select one to use with children in your church or home. Consider using the "Big Picture Questions and Answers for Kids" as a catechism. These questions and answers are available in Lifeway's Gospel Project curriculum.
- Consider introducing the idea of using catechisms to parents in various training opportunities, such as parenting seminars, parent/child dedication classes, or covenant membership classes.
- Explore opportunities in corporate worship services to incorporate the practice of questions and answers.

CHAPTER 11

Generational Discipleship Among Spiritual Orphans

Ron Hunter Jr.

Do you realize how many stories and movies feature famous characters who were orphans? Charles Dickens described the self-reflection of Pip in *Great Expectations*. Mark Twain took us on an adventure with Tom Sawyer. Other orphans like J. M. Barrie's Peter Pan, Brontë's Jane Eyre, and Victor Hugo's Cosette jumped off the pages of nineteenth-century literature. If movies seem more exciting than novels, look no further than the orphaned heroes Superman, Iron Man, Cinderella, Snow White, Tarzan, Luke Skywalker, and his sister Leia. Everyone remembers feeling strong emotion when Mufasa died, leaving Simba to navigate the wiles of becoming king of the pride without the guidance of his father.

While society cheers for orphans in the fictional world, few rally around real-life children who need spiritual guidance from parents or other adults. The excitement and mystique of Luke Skywalker or Clark Kent fade when you realize you may be needed as Luke's Obi-Wan Kenobi or Clark's Jonathan and Martha Kent. Everyone wants to be the transformed hero without doing the hard work of investing in their transformation. An orphan's greatest need beyond finding Christ is a warm, nurturing adult who will invest time and mentoring in his or her life. The Bible vividly depicts orphans transforming into heroes under the guidance of mentors. Both roles, the orphan and the mentor, offer vital redemptive insights into pivotal moments of salvation and transformation. Without an invested adult who engages the child, that little one will be less likely to find Christ or see his or her grand plan within God's story. This chapter delves into the transformative journeys of biblical orphans by uncovering principles and practices that guided them to faithfully following Christ into adulthood and shows you how to invest in children.

Family Ministry and Orphans

In recent years, children's and student ministry have begun to morph into intergenerational connections emphasizing family ministry. But what defines family ministry? What is family? Would the child who attends your church alone feel like part of the church family? Circumstances, even in church, can change perceptions, causing children to feel left out or like strangers in a foreign land. Would Joseph, sold into slavery by his brothers, taken from his father, and exiled to another country, still see himself as family? What about the young newlywed Ruth, whose husband died? Children who come to salvation most often do so because of an influential person who made a connection in their lives. If that connecting person is not a parent, the task of reaching the child becomes harder. The implications of all these dynamics show why most churches have strategically shifted toward family ministry over the last two decades. Consequently, churches must avoid seeing family ministry through rose-colored glasses and instead view it as the biblical redemptive calling of generational discipleship.

Family Ministry

Avoid the flawed perspective that family ministry suggests a church structure programmed for homes that have two parents, two children, and a picket fence. Damage and deep-seated scars can result from the perception that family ministry only includes those with one or more biological relatives, preferably children living under their roof. What about couples whose children are grown, couples who have no children, young unmarried couples, those who never married, and various other typical situations? Make sure that your family ministry, or any ministry, does not exclude these life situations. Family is messy, because marriage takes work and because raising children is hard work. Christian spouses argue, have problems, and file for divorce. However, Christians have considerably lower divorce rates than unbelievers.[1] In fact, Shaunti Feldhahn documented happier marriages for those who are active in church. While marriage is often the foundation or source of family, people who are family may not marry. Not everyone chooses marriage, and not all marriages

---

[1] Shaunti Feldhahn, "Divorce Rates are Not What You Think They Are!" Shaunti Feldhahn (May 27, 2021), https://shaunti.com/2021/05/divorce-rates-are-not-what-you-think-they-are/.

produce children. As a result, family ministries should not narrow the goal audience to exclude others who biblically and practically fit within the definition of "family."

Marriage is not a criterion for family today or in Scripture. A person's role can fit biologically within a family without the person ever being married, as with a son, daughter, sister, brother, uncle, or aunt. Without violating one's convictions, family can be defined beyond biology. "Scripture explains that upon embracing faith, **one finds his or her place in God's family, a bond stronger than biology**, where we are **all His children, adopted into a divine kinship**."[2] Even outside of biology or Christianity, you see bonds that many describe as family within the workplace, the military, law enforcement, and other affinity groups. The definition of "family" is people who share a common interest or experience by either biological or relational means.[3] The definition is of "family," not "family ministry" or "marriage." The broadness of the definition is not meant to be exclusively Christian, because if a Christian's son or daughter embraces a sinful lifestyle and walks away from Christianity and church, those parents and their children are still family.

Church leaders need to acknowledge the diversity in family structures, including the young widow with two children; the single dad trying to hold it together; the abandoned child with identity struggles; and the orphan, whether physical or spiritual. Some churches use language like "home ministry" to prevent excluding numerous situations. Looking at the broad scope of who people consider family, a task that is different from defining biblical marriage,

---

[2] Ron Hunter Jr., "Beyond Biology: A Portrait of Family," *ONE Magazine: One Lord, One Voice, One Vision* 20, no. 3 (April-May 2024), 9. Emphasis in original.

[3] Hunter, 8–9.

then "family ministry" opens a wide-ranging set of relationships the church is called to reach for Christ and disciple. Family ministry goes beyond catering to families that fit a traditional mold; it assumes roles beyond biological ties such as mentor, teacher, bonus parent, and friend.

The teachings of Deuteronomy 6 emphasize parental, generational, and communal responsibility to nurture faith across all ages. Verse 3 of chapter 6 begins with "Hear O Israel," and this is repeated in verse 4 as God, through Moses, addresses the community before talking to parents and grandparents. Eugene Merrill said that Deuteronomy 6, the Shema, was a "covenant . . . made with the nation as a whole"[4] and that "the singular form of the verb [to hear] emphasizes the corporate or collective nature of the addressee,"[5] indicating a group larger than the nuclear or biological family. The collective community is composed of Christ-followers who look for children without godly influences and of parents who impart biblical values. This body of believers forms God's family, creating a spiritual lineage enriched by members of a faith community—spiritual brothers and sisters. Your commission from Christ is to reach the people who are not part of his family.

To further reinforce that family extends beyond biology even outside Christianity, think about how you may feel closer to people within affinity groups than to your biological family. People with whom you spend time and in whom you place trust, such as coworkers, fellow athletes, church friends, and fellow soldiers, can all feel closer than actual family. Children in our churches may have uninvolved parents who are one or more of the following: distant,

---

[4] Eugene Merrill, *Deuteronomy*, NAC 4 (B&H, 1994), 162.

[5] Merrill, 162.

addicted, incarcerated, abusive, or caught up in negative circumstances, creating orphan-like children. Children and teens in such disconnected situations may gravitate to a children's minister, youth pastor, Sunday school teacher, or even the parent of one of their friends. Now for a more sobering question: What about the child who has parents who come to church with them but are spiritually uninvolved? The same disconnection shows up in a spiritually absent parent whose faith-value consequences differ little from those of a physically absent parent. You will find both physical and spiritual orphans in your church.

Orphans

Technically, the word "orphan" describes a child whose parents have died. The orphan category expands beyond the traditional definition in the negative consequences of losing parents to death, as mentioned earlier in this chapter. The population of this spiritual orphan group within your ministry may surprise you. Cheryl Nixon goes further in the *Oxford Bibliographies* to define an orphan as "a child who has been deprived of parental care and has not been adopted."[6] Numerous children have been deprived of faith values from their parents, even when they attend church as a nuclear family. Workaholic parents make orphan-like children who may feel more resentment than children who lost their parents to death. Ministry has made orphans of many pastors' children. As you consider the topic of salvation and children, ask how you will reach and disciple the ones with

[6] Cheryl Nixon, *Orphan*, Oxford Bibliographies (2013), https://www.oxfordbibliographies.com/display/document/obo-9780199791231/obo-9780199791231-0121.xml.

little to no Christian influence in the home without someone adopting through a mentoring relationship.

When Christians step into orphan-like situations, they are figuratively adopting the spiritually neglected children. Within this chapter, the word "adopted" refers not to legal adoption but to spiritual adoption in the form of showing interest that results in mentoring toward Christlike discipleship or in spiritual parenting in the absence of a spiritually involved parent. Adoption and spiritual parenting will be used interchangeably in this chapter. Scripture calls the community to recognize the need to step in when no parent or no spiritual parent provides that needed generational discipleship (Deut 6:4–9; Titus 2; 2 Timothy 1).

A spiritually orphaned child is defined as a child who either has no parent or has no Christian parent who intentionally and consistently provides Christlike influence and encourages God's will through regular conversations and meaningful connections. A spiritually absent parent offers very little extra consolation over a physically absent parent. The family who walks in on Sunday mornings, sits together, smiles, and even volunteers may very well be the one who never interacts outside the church with faith conversations. Well-meaning parents provide rides to practices, clothing, cleats, instruments, and more, thinking all their child's "needs" are met and neglecting godly insights and consistent discipleship. Those same responsible parents expect the church to provide their children with faith values.

Just as orphans need legal guardians and as spiritual orphans need spiritual guardians, spiritually orphaned children need someone to show concern, have conversations with them, and get involved. The conversations cannot be solely lectures or correction, as these deprived children hear that tone all too often. Spiritual orphans need someone to ask who they are, what their story is, what matters to them, and what they spend time thinking about. Unless these lonely children can relate to you, they will not listen to you. And without sincere concern, you will have no influence.

Most people who rose above their difficulties can easily name five to ten people who were influential in connecting with them during that time. When it comes to helping children find Christ and discipling them, it still takes a "great cloud of witnesses" (Heb 12:1 NIV) who serve as examples, mentors, or teachers. Hebrews 11 describes ordinary, dysfunctional people who had influences in their lives to do something great for God. These misfits, several of whom were orphans, are included in the great faith chapter of the Bible because someone or several people poured into them. How well is the church continuing the legacy of generational discipleship beyond biology?

Biblical Orphans

This chapter began with examples of famous orphans from literature and movies, but the Bible also contains accounts of well-known orphans. People often study the great characters of Scripture without considering how others stepped into their lives in intentional and redeeming ways. Just as Luke Skywalker had Obi-Wan and Yoda, Scripture's Timothy had Paul; Esther had Mordecai. You may never have considered Daniel as an orphan, but his exile to Babylon immediately changed his status. Daniel's friends Shadrach, Meshach, and Abednego earned hero-like status when standing firm in a hostile Babylonian culture. Their unnamed parents had prepared them well. Esther's cousin Mordecai influenced her teenage years and helped her rescue the Hebrew people from genocide. You can easily see mentors of biblical greats in the story of God's redemptive plan.

Look more closely at familiar stories whose lead characters were biblical orphans.

A young lady married into a family of a different nationality. While Scripture does not indicate much about her new husband or father-in-law, it does speak of her mother-in-law. Through her new family, she was introduced to God. While the details are unclear, this young woman and the mother-in-law both tragically lost their husbands in close succession. Naomi shared experiences with Ruth during the ten years Ruth was married to her son, and their connection grew. Ruth, now without her own family, found a connection with her mother-in-law, Naomi, and with her God. As Naomi prepared to return to her native Bethlehem, she advised Ruth to stay in Moab so she could remarry within her own people. Because Naomi and Ruth truly connected through everyday experiences, Ruth sacrificed residency in her homeland to become the foreigner with Naomi.[7]

Her passion and powerful connection to her mentor are evident as Ruth declared, "Don't plead with me to abandon you or to return and not follow you. For wherever you go, I will go, and wherever you live, I will live; your people will be my people, and your God will be my God. Where you die, I will die, and there I will be buried. May the Lord punish me, and do so severely, if anything but death separates you and me" (Ruth 1:16–17). Block explained that Ruth's pledge included "the adoption of the other person's family and faith as one's own."[8] Naomi took Ruth under her wing, even though Ruth was a generation younger. Subsequently, Ruth adopted Naomi back. Naomi's selfless investment in Ruth during her own time of deep grief and distraction resulted in Ruth becoming one of

---

[7] Daniel Block, *Judges, Ruth*, NAC 6 (B&H, 1999), 643.

[8] Block, 643.

the five women named in Christ's genealogy and led to the story of the kinsman redeemer.

Another young lady found herself in a precarious situation. Her beauty caught the attention of the ruling king, as did others he was considering for his soon-to-be new queen. Unbeknownst to the king, this young lady was Jewish, and she was part of the conquered people in subjection. Her name was Esther, and she had been orphaned twice (Esth 2:7–8): first when her parents died and again when the king took her from Mordecai and placed her with Hegai.[9] Her cousin Mordecai had stepped in as a father figure advising her.

After Esther became queen, a side plot formed. A self-centered, narcissistic advisor of the king named Haman duped the king into signing a decree (which is binding and irrevocable), allowing for the mass genocide of all the Jews for a brief season. Imagine the movie *The Purge* but with the open season of killing directed at only the Jews, who up to this point, as in the movie, have been everyone's good neighbors. Mordecai advised and helped build Esther's confidence to stand for her convictions, even in tough situations. She needed to protect her people, even though, as the queen, she might have gone undetected as a target of the decree. Mordecai led, advised, and reminded Esther of her roots at various moments.[10] Mordecai's wisdom and teaching allowed this orphan to rise to the second highest power in the land "for such a time as this" (4:14). Esther listened, learned, and adopted the convictions of her mentor Mordecai as she mustered the courage to approach the king, reveal her own ethnicity, uncover the plot of Haman, and offer a plan to protect the Jews.

---

[9] Marion Taylor, *Ruth, Esther*, The Story of God Bible Commentary (Zondervan, 2020), 120.

[10] Debra Reid, *Esther: An Introduction and Commentary*, TOTC 13 (IVP, 2008) 39, 104.

What a story as Esther went from timid to bold when she courageously said, "I will risk my position, my life, and all the luxuries to do what is right, and if I die, I die." You never know the impact of a mentored life, especially when helping young children and teens find their moral and spiritual footing.

Four more standout orphans showed up in Babylon after Judah had been conquered and many young people had been taken away for training and enculturation. Daniel, Shadrach, Meshach, and Abednego (as they are affectionately known when mixing Hebrew and Babylonian names) underwent the equivalent of a bachelor's education at a residential college. Daniel 1:5 says they learned and trained for three years; without summers off, that time equals a modern four-year degree. The king's intent was to transform their mindset and worldview from Jewish to Babylonian. The time away from home in college is the second most influential period of a person's life when a major shift of values occurs. These four orphans might have felt abandoned by God and could have justified abandoning their childhood values taught by their parents before exile.

How did Daniel and his three friends not fall under the influence of a hostile Babylonian culture? These four had godly parents and teachers who established strong values during their childhood and early teenage years. When they had the freedom to make their own choices, they still chose a godly path. Similarly, graduating seniors move from a structured high-school schedule to college classes with more free time than previously experienced. If undisciplined, their studies and life choices can suffer. The word "undisciplined" is key; a discipled child often possesses discipline and a less self-centered worldview.

While the OT is rife with orphan stories and mentors, some had more success than others. Only some get an Elisha or Samuel to mentor. Abraham tried mentoring Lot with little success. As in biblical times, not everyone will receive counsel and follow God's direction when you attempt to mentor and disciple them.

Moving to the NT, examine one more spiritual orphan. Timothy had a godly mother and grandmother, Eunice and Lois, who were Jewish believers (2 Tim 1:5). His father was Greek and likely an unbeliever. Paul identified Timothy's godly heritage from the matriarchal side, omitting any influence of his father. Paul further identified Timothy as his "true son" (1 Tim 1:2) and his "dearly loved son" (2 Tim 1:2), taking the role of spiritual, nurturing mentor as he discipled him into a great leader. Paul took Timothy on journeys, wrote him letters, and treated him like a son. Timothy learned from Paul, building on the foundation set by his mother and grandmother. But lacking a spiritual biological father, Timothy adopted Paul and his passion for church planting.

While Timothy was not a true orphan, his situation does fit the adoption category because another adult stepped into the gap of a missing father figure and was intentional about nurturing his walk with Christ. Paul, like adults today, could mentor more than one younger person. In addition to Timothy, Paul mentored Titus, whom he also called "son," (Titus 1:4) and John Mark, who once frustrated Paul but was given a second chance. Imagine the children in your church, neighborhoods, sports leagues, and musical groups who could be young Esthers, Timothys, Daniels, or Ruths. Imagine the impact mentoring could have and how life altering it could be for their future children and the generations who follow.

Children might find spiritual guidance in the unlikeliest mentors; family ministry should expand to fill these necessary roles. As you have seen, the OT and NT reveal spiritual orphans needing mentors to spiritually parent them. Mordecai counseled his cousin

Esther, and Paul adopted Timothy and Titus as his sons in the faith. These biblical roles went beyond parental and biological relationships to an influence that made a significant difference. Likewise, you must think beyond the salvation decision to provide discipleship-style mentoring to children and teens who could change their generational legacy.

Mentoring forms a framework for discipleship and appears frequently within Scripture. Joy Jones-Carmack did extensive study in this area and showed how Moses mentored the Israelites even as Jethro mentored him. You can see positive mentoring and the consequences of no mentoring as "Exodus 18 and Judges 2 provide further insight into the distinction between mentoring and discipling. Exodus 18 demonstrates the benefits of mentoring and discipling, while Judges 2 illustrates the dangers of neglecting these behaviors."[11] The same can be said of the churches today who think discipleship happens only through sermons and lessons at church. Lifelong values are taught in the rhythm and routine of everyday life, just as one learns to love sports, journaling, reading, hiking, or art through someone who took the time to talk about these interests. When children have an adult mentor talking to them about Christ and Scripture daily, they are less likely to abandon their faith. Children will adopt the values of those they trust and respect; therefore, biblical worldviews can be established by mentors. The Barna Group found that 64 percent of children who grow up in church will walk away from

---

[11] Joy Jones-Carmack, "Understanding Discipling and Mentoring Through an Exegetical Analysis of Exodus 18:13–23 and Judges 2:6–17," *Journal of Applied Christian Leadership* (Sep. 1, 2021), https://jacl.andrews.edu/understanding-discipling-and-mentoring-through-an-exegetical-analysis-of-exodus-1813-23-and-judges-26-17.

their faith and church, often becoming prodigals.[12] How many of the 64 percent lacked an adult spiritual mentor to adopt them outside of church? Spiritual orphans need one or more invested and involved godly mentors.

Discipleship Principles for Orphans and Spiritual Orphans

Discipleship Requires a Connected Relationship with a Christ Focus

People go to restaurants or make purchases based on ratings and likes, a tendency that reveals choices based on trust of others over the institution. Children will come to church based on relationships: a friend, parent, grandparent, or teacher who invests in them. Once a connection is made, then discipleship takes on a spiritually focused form of mentoring.[13] Before someone allows you to disciple him or her, that person will need to see you as a mentor, even subconsciously. Most cannot transition from acquaintance to serious discipleship quickly. Be patient, as they may push you away initially. But with graceful persistence and curiously asked questions, you can transform a causal relationship into a life-changing one.

To disciple a child or adult, you must consistently follow Christ. The mentoring or generational discipleship chapter, Deuteronomy 6,

---

[12] "Church Dropouts Have Risen to 64%—But What About Those Who Stay?" Barna Group (Sep. 4, 2019), https://www.barna.com/research/resilient-disciples/.

[13] Desmond Gaius Boldeau, "Developing a Mentoring Model, Based on Christ's Approach to Discipleship, for Intern Pastors in the British Union" (PhD diss., Andrews University, 2004), 80, 89, 98–99.

begins with a declaration followed by a command. When you declare the Lord is our God (Deut 6:4), children will detect whether your Christianity is authentic or a Sunday-only posture. The good news is that orphans truly want a trusted influence in their lives; the bad news is that orphans, who feel abandoned, may not easily build trust with healthy potential influences.

Spiritual Orphans Need Discipling, Nurturing Figures in Their Lives

Vern Bengtson conducted the most thorough, long-term study on faith retention from childhood to adulthood and discovered that a warm, nurturing father was the number one influential factor.[14] Ephesians 6:4 singles out fathers and calls them to "nurture" (KJV) in regard to their children, a command that may not come as naturally for fathers as it does for mothers. While other translations change the word nurture, the context and meaning call fathers to educate, train, discipline, and instruct. Another study reinforced Bengtson's warm, nurturing fathers concept but expanded his research and found that parents who routinely engaged in two-way faith conversations with their children during the week overwhelmingly saw an increase in their children's faith formation.[15] Sadly, orphans, physical or spiritual, miss the primary influences of a warm, nurturing father and the engaging faith conversations of Christian parents.

---

[14] Vern Bengtson, *Families and Faith: How Religion is Passed Down Across Generations* (Oxford University Press, 2013), 76–79, 196.

[15] Christian Smith and Amy Adamczyk, *Handing Down the Faith: How Parents Pass Their Religion on to the Next Generation* (Oxford University Press, 2021), 69–70.

Just as nineteenth-century scientists discovered that sterilizing surgical instruments increases the survival rate by reducing infection, the church should encourage faith conversations in the homes and among spiritual orphans by recruiting and training more adults.

Potential mentors need guidance and tools to help discuss faith and Scripture. Most parents who fail to disciple their children are poor disciples themselves. When the church helps parents nurture their own biblical worldview, then these parents can counsel their children on everyday decisions based on Scripture. When parents engage their own children, often their children's friends benefit as well. Did you catch that? Nurturing parents naturally mentor more children than their own. The same nurturing parents could be your best trainers for other parents. Nurturing parents step into orphan-like situations to make a difference, just like the mentors from the OT and NT.

Nurturing Mentors Adopt Spiritual Orphans

Chap Clark, who may be the key thought leader on adoptive discipleship, explained how family is bigger than biology when saying, "We must commit to making sure every young person knows that they matter not only to God but to a large and diverse family because God *and his church* declare it so."[16] Richard Ross also described how teens feel valued when adults unrelated to them show interest and invest in their development, and such relationships allow for biblical worldview development.[17] Spiritual parenting includes being involved

---

[16] Chap Clark, "The Adoption View of Youth Ministry," in *Youth Ministry in the 21st century: Five views*, ed. Chap Clark (Baker Academic, 2015), 85.

[17] Richard Ross, "Youth Ministry in Thirds," in *Recalibrate: A New Measure for Family Ministry*, ed. Ron Hunter Jr. (Randall House, 2019),

in a child's or a teenager's life, and more than one conversation or shared moment is required for them to notice and feel the dedicated concern and love for them.

Children who grow up staying faithful in their walk with Christ can look back and identify pivotal adult relationships that influenced their moral and Christian decision-making. Children who take an interest in Christ have Christian adults taking an interest in them. Never underestimate the value of praying adults who adopt a child or teen for whom they pray. When you pray, the generational differences or preferences that previously irritated you no longer keep you apart. Nurturing mentors include Sunday school teachers, children's ministers, student pastors, key volunteers, a friend's parents, coaches, and other individuals that interact in the lives of young developing children. Karen Kennemur reminded ministry leaders, "The church that partners with parents strengthens the faith walk of the entire family,"[18] and the same can be said of partnering with spiritual parents of spiritual orphans. You need to teach other adults to step into the lives of their children's friends or volunteer in children's ministry to build influential relationships with children who need a safe, godly, nurturing adult. Identifying spiritual orphans within your church pinpoints immediate opportunities, but nurturing those who could nurture charts a path for real investment in adolescent lives.

123–26.

[18] Karen Kennemur, "Nurturing Faith in the Home: Equipping Parents of Children to Be Spiritual Leaders" in *Family Ministry and the Church: A Leader's Guide for Ministry Through Families*, ed. Chris Shirley (Randall House, 2018), 175.

Use or Develop Simple Surveys to Determine the Efficacy of Churched Adults in Generational Discipleship

You can survey your church to determine what percentage of people talk about lessons from small groups or Sunday school with their children or have any faith conversation in the home. You might be surprised at how low the percentages are. A poor result typically means there are parents and adults who do not know why or how to have routine faith conversations. Parents only know to do what they saw in their own parents unless coached to do better. Similarly, adults will be intentional only when taught how to be intentional. Surveys often instruct as well as measure. For example, when you ask how many engage or mentor children who are not biologically related, it makes the adult more aware of what is expected.

Find Tools That Help Adults Start Conversations That Connect and Then Lead to Involvement in the Child's Life

After teaching adults the how and why of mentoring spiritual orphans, make it stick by providing a tool that gives them easy wins. Faith conversations do not include a lecture or corrections, nor are they formal lessons, but they are, rather, dialogue in which you ask the child questions and listen. The Shema provides a community framework—"Hear, O Israel" (Deut 6:4, c.f. 6:3 NIV)—calling for everyone to take part. These verses would become the most recited and sacred in all Scripture for the Jewish community and, as such, should have bearing for us today. In fact, Duane Christensen calls the Shema and the directives contained in the Shema verses "a pedagogical tool to instruct each generation."[19] In the task of instructing, tools help both teacher and student learn and remember the lesson, the same way Jesus taught visually using parables. Tools can include experiences, discussion questions, devotional readings, curriculum (which is the truest form of pedagogy), and other resources. Adults who step into the role of mentor or spiritual parent need tools to learn and teach beyond their favorite topics or repertoire of knowledge.

Make Sure Mentors Maintain Safe Boundaries

Remind the mentors that children whose parents play no active spiritual role should not feel threatened or shamed by the adult who takes an interest in teaching them. Teach intentionality by pinpointing and addressing the needs of each child or teenager. If the mentor can befriend the spiritual orphan's parent, both the child and the parent might be developed. Obviously, background checks should be conducted on all volunteers in your church, especially ones who interact with minors. Can you have non-Christians as mentors? If the goal in mentoring spiritual orphans is to win them to Christ while helping them develop a biblical worldview, the answer is no.

Remember, Above All, You Serve a God of Redemption

Until Christ returns, humans remain flawed, and spiritual orphans will exist. Such children need mentors who will spiritually parent them by intentionally investing in them. You cannot forget that "God wants the church to help shape the home—even if broken or

---

[19] Duane Christensen, *Deuteronomy 1–21:9*, 2nd ed., WBC 6a (Thomas Nelson, 2001), 137.

damaged—into what He intends."[20] You serve in ministry as paid staff or as a volunteer because God chose or adopted you. You mentor because others mentored and influenced you. You serve in ministry to put Barna out of the business of reporting unhealthy statistical patterns. Imagine no longer reading about how many children walk away from church or their faith. Because we live in a fallen world, we need Barna to remind us of the urgent need to reach and teach. Generational discipleship is salvation and mentoring that reaches all ages, regardless of marital or parenting status or of intact, broken, or shattered homes. Ministry should create mentoring connections that disciple and invest in those who need it most. Let us reduce the number of spiritual orphans who need someone to mentor and spiritually parent them as described in Deuteronomy 6; Titus 2; and 2 Timothy 1. Identify the young Daniels, Esthers, and Timothys in your church.

Discussion Questions

1. Identify and analyze the stories of orphans in the Bible mentioned in the chapter, such as Ruth, Esther, Daniel, and Timothy. How did their mentors influence their spiritual and personal developments? What lessons can be drawn from these relationships for modern-day discipleship?
2. What are the unique challenges faced by spiritual orphans, as outlined in the chapter? How can church communities effectively identify and support children who fall into this category?

---

[20] Ron Hunter Jr., *The DNA of D6: Building Blocks of Generational Discipleship* (Randall House, 2015), 4.

3. Analyze the importance of generational discipleship in the context of Deuteronomy 6 and other biblical passages. How does this approach differ from more traditional methods of discipleship?
4. Reflect on your own experiences with mentorship and discipleship. Have you ever had a mentor who played a significant role in your spiritual growth?

Opportunities for Application

- Applying the principles from this chapter, brainstorm and write out three of four ways to become a mentor for others. Review the footnotes of this chapter for helpful resources or discuss mentorship opportunities with a ministry leader at your church.
- This chapter emphasizes the need for practical tools and training for mentors so children can find salvation. Work with leaders in your church to discover the kinds of resources and support systems your church might provide to equip mentors for their roles in spiritual parenting with biological and spiritually adopted children.
- Examine the ministry opportunities and programming your church provides. Does it most often assume a two-parent household? Look through recent and upcoming publications to identify ways to include single-parent homes, families with disabilities, or children and students who do not live with a parent. Identify and mentor children without Christian influence (spiritual orphans) in their homes. Look for ways to include single parents and their children

in corporate worship or other church programming, including special events such as Easter or Christmas services. Single parents or parents with children with disabilities are sometimes overlooked for ministry service opportunities. Consider requesting their input, if not their involvement, in ministry planning assignments.

- Maintaining appropriate boundaries and following church safety and privacy policies, consider forming a small ministry team for each age group to identify preschoolers, children, and students in your church who may not have spiritual guidance at home. Write out ways to include those boys and girls in activities and opportunities for spiritual growth and discipleship.

CONTRIBUTORS

David S. Dockery, PhD, Distinguished Professor of Theology, Southwestern Baptist Theological Seminary

W. Madison Grace II, PhD, Associate Professor of Theology, Southwestern Baptist Theological Seminary

Adam Harwood, PhD, Professor of Theology, New Orleans Baptist Theological Seminary

Ron Hunter Jr., PhD, Executive Director of D6 and Randall House Publishers, Adjunct Professor, Dallas Baptist University

Karen Kennemur, PhD, Professor of Children's Ministry, Southwestern Baptist Theological Seminary

Shelly Melia, PhD, Professor of Childhood Education, Dallas Baptist University

Donna B. Peavey, PhD, Professor of Christian Education New Orleans Baptist Theological Seminary

Sandra Peoples, PhD Candidate, Instructor, John W. Rawlings School of Divinity

James R. Wicker, PhD, Professor of New Testament, Southwestern Baptist Theological Seminary

Joshua E. Williams, PhD, Associate Professor of Old Testament, Southwestern Baptist Theological Seminary

Malcolm B. Yarnell III, PhD, Research Professor of Theology, Southwestern Baptist Theological Seminary

GENERAL INDEX

T

SCRIPTURE INDEX

1 Corinthians

2 Corinthians

Galatians

Ephesians

Philippians

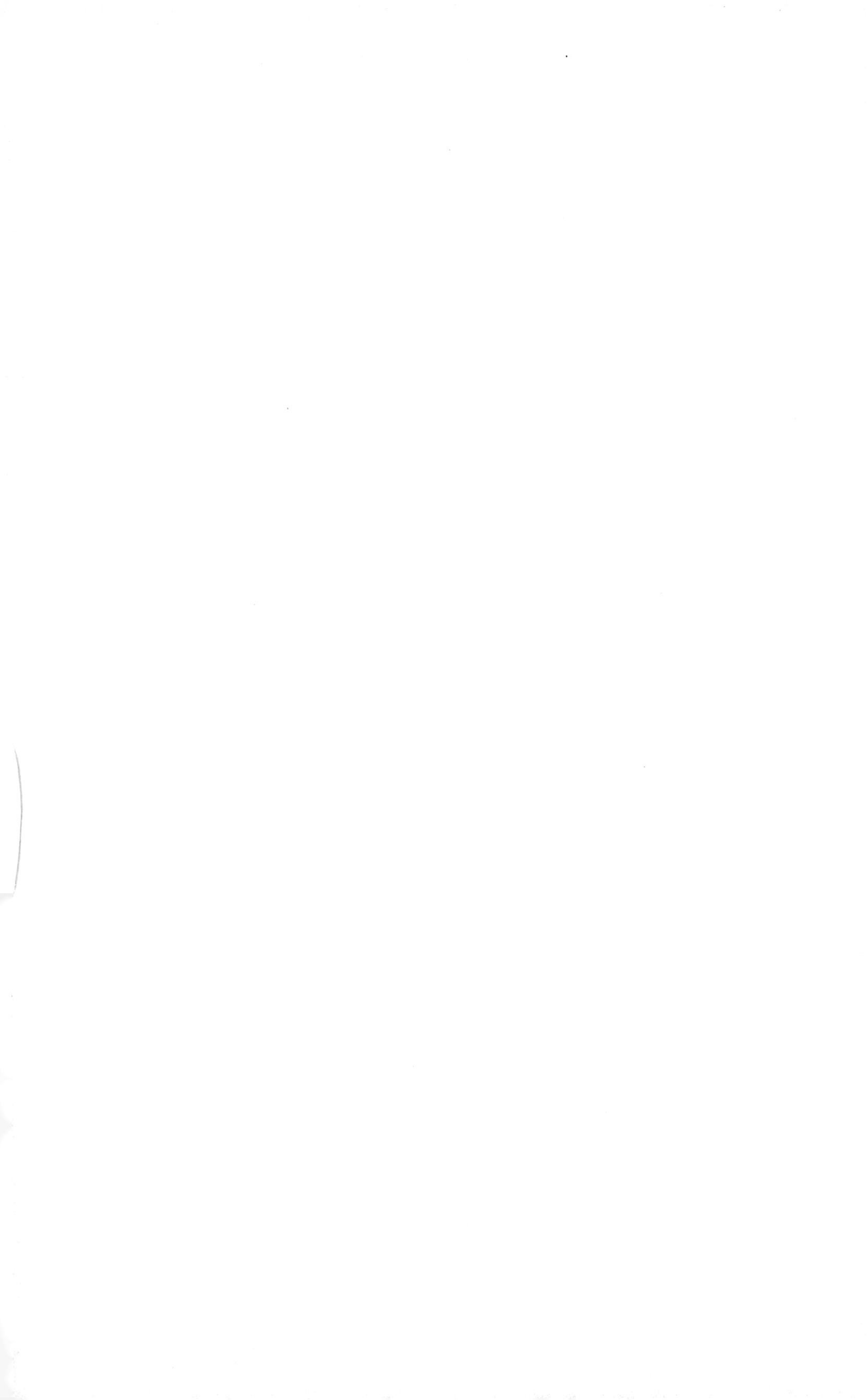